Accumula 6

STUDENT BOOK

T0283637

JUMP Math
One Yonge Street, Suite 1014
Toronto, Ontario M5E 1E5
Canada
www.jumpmath.org

Writers: Dr. John Mighton, Dr. Sindi Sabourin, Dr. Anna Klebanov, Dr. Sohrab Rahbar, Julie Lorinc, Dr. Heather Betel
Editors: Dishpreet Kaur, Dimitra Chronopoulos, Debbie Davies-Wright, Ewa Krynski
Layout and Illustrations: Linh Lam, Gabriella Kerr
Cover Design: Sunday Lek
Cover Photograph: © alexokov/Freepik.com

ISBN 978-1-77395-298-7

First printing January 2024

Parts of this material were first published in 2013 in AP Book 6.1, US edition (978-1-927457-06-1) and AP Book 6.2, US edition (978-1-927457-07-8).

Printed and bound in Canada

Welcome to JUMP Math!

Entering the world of JUMP Math means believing that every learner has the capacity to be fully numerate and love math.

The **JUMP Math Accumula Student Book** is the companion to the **JUMP Math Accumula** supplementary resource for Grades 1 to 8, which is designed to strengthen foundational math knowledge and prepare all students for success in understanding math problems at grade level. This book provides opportunities for students to consolidate learning by exploring important math concepts through independent practice.

Unique Evidence-Based Approach and Resources

JUMP Math's unique approach, Kindergarten to Grade 8 resources, and professional learning for teachers have been producing positive learning outcomes for children and teachers in classrooms in Canada, the United States, and other countries for over 20 years. Our resources are aligned with the science on how children's brains learn best and have been demonstrated through studies to greatly improve problem solving, computation, and fluency skills. (See our research at **jumpmath.org**.) Our approach is designed to build equity by supporting the full spectrum of learners to achieve success in math.

Confidence Building is Key

JUMP Math begins each grade with review to enable every student to quickly develop the confidence needed to engage deeply with math. Our distinctive incremental approach to learning math concepts gradually increases the level of difficulty for students, empowering them to become motivated, independent problem solvers. Our books are also designed with simple pictures and models to avoid overwhelming learners when introducing new concepts, enabling them to see the deep structure of the math and gain the confidence to solve a wide range of math problems.

About JUMP Math

JUMP Math is a non-profit organization dedicated to helping every child in every classroom develop confidence, understanding, and a love of math. JUMP Math also offers a comprehensive set of classroom resources for students in Kindergarten to Grade 8.

For more information, visit JUMP Math at: www.jumpmath.org.

Contents

1. Multiplying and Dividing by Skip Counting

Amy finds the product of **3** and **5** by skip counting on a number line. She counts off three 5s. From the picture, Amy can see that the **product** of 3 and 5 is 15.

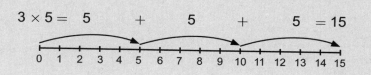

1. Draw arrows to find the product by skip counting.

   a) **4 × 2 =**

   b) **3 × 4 =**

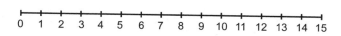   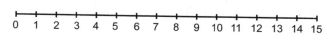

2. Use the number line to skip count by 4s, 6s, and 7s. Fill in the boxes below as you count.

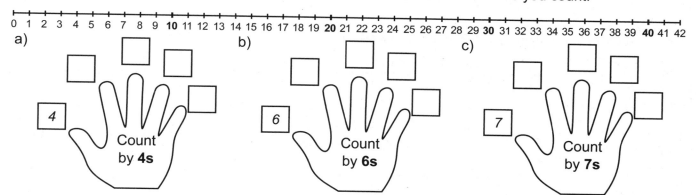

3. Find the product by skip counting on your fingers. Use the hands from Question 2 to help:

 7   14   21   28

   a) 3 × 5 =   b) 5 × 2 =   c) 3 × 4 =   d) 3 × 6 =   e) 1 × 7 =

   f) 3 × 7 =   g) 3 × 3 =   h) 6 × 1 =   i) 2 × 7 =   j) 5 × 5 =

   k) 2 × 2 =   l) 7 × 1 =   m) 4 × 4 =   n) 4 × 6 =   o) 1 × 6 =

4. Find the number of items in each picture. Write a multiplication statement for each picture.

   a)

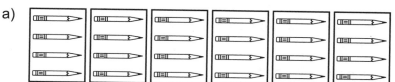

   b)

You can solve the division problem **12 ÷ 4 = ?** by skip counting on a number line.

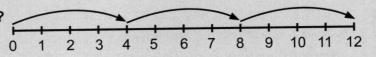

The number line shows that it takes three skips of size 4 to get 12.

$$4 + 4 + 4 = 12 \quad \text{so} \quad 12 \div 4 = 3$$

5. Use the number line to find the answer to the division problem. Be sure to draw arrows to show your skip counting.

a)
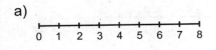

8 ÷ 2 = _____

b)
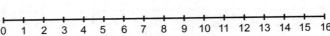

16 ÷ 8 = _____

6. What division equation does the picture represent?

a)
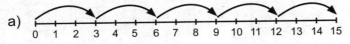

_____

b)
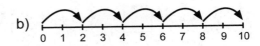

_____

You can also find the answer to a division question by skip counting on your fingers.

For example, to find **45 ÷ 9**, count by 9s until you reach 45. The number of fingers you have up when you say "45" is the answer.

9   18   27   36   45

So **45 ÷ 9 = 5**

7. Find the answer by skip counting on your fingers.

a) 35 ÷ 5 = ____   b) 12 ÷ 6 = ____   c) 32 ÷ 8 = ____   d) 21 ÷ 7 = ____   e) 45 ÷ 5 = ____

f) 36 ÷ 4 = ____   g) 25 ÷ 5 = ____   h) 42 ÷ 6 = ____   i) 27 ÷ 3 = ____   j) 16 ÷ 2 = ____

k) 36 ÷ 6 = ____   l) 35 ÷ 7 = ____   m) 18 ÷ 3 = ____   n) 21 ÷ 3 = ____   o) 40 ÷ 8 = ____

8. There are 24 flowers in 6 bouquets. How many flowers are in each bouquet? _____

9. 36 trees are in 9 rows. How many trees are in each row? _____

10. Amy uses 8 pencils in a month. How many months will she take to use 32 pencils? _____

2. Mental Math and the Standard Method for Multiplication

This is how Leela multiplies **4 × 22**:

She rewrites 22 as a sum:	$22 = 20 + 2$
She multiplies 4 by 20:	$4 \times 20 = 80$
She multiplies 4 by 2:	$4 \times 2 = 8$
She adds the two results:	$80 + 8 = 88$

Leela concludes that **4 × 22 = 88.**

This picture shows why Leela's method works:

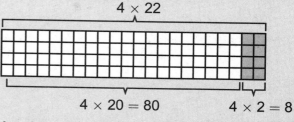

$4 \times 20 = 80 \qquad 4 \times 2 = 8$

$$4 \times 22 = (4 \times 20) + (4 \times 2) = 80 + 8 = 88$$

1. Use the picture to write the multiplication expression as a sum.

a)

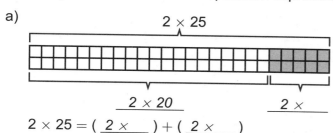

2×20 $2 \times$ _____

$2 \times 25 = ($ __2 ×__ $) + ($ __2 ×__ $)$

b) 3×15

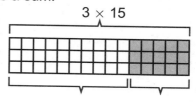

_____   _____

$3 \times 15 = ($ _____ $) + ($ _____ $)$

2. Multiply using Leela's method.

a) $5 \times 13 = $ ___5 × 10___ $+$ ___5 × 3___ $= $ ___50 + 15___ $= $ _____65_____

b) $4 \times 21 = $ _____ $+$ _____ $=$ _____ $=$ _____

c) $3 \times 43 = $ _____ $+$ _____ $=$ _____ $=$ _____

d) $2 \times 432 = $ __2 × 400__ $+$ __2 × 30__ $+$ __2 × 2__ $=$ __800 + 60 + 4__ $=$ __864__

e) $3 \times 312 = $ _____ $+$ _____ $+$ _____ $=$ _____ $=$ _____

f) $4 \times 321 = $ _____ $+$ _____ $+$ _____ $=$ _____ $=$ _____

3. Multiply in your head by multiplying the digits separately.

a) $3 \times 12 = $ _____   b) $3 \times 52 = $ _____   c) $6 \times 31 = $ _____   d) $7 \times 21 = $ _____

e) $5 \times 31 = $ _____   f) $3 \times 42 = $ _____   g) $6 \times 51 = $ _____   h) $2 \times 44 = $ _____

i) $4 \times 521 = $ _____   j) $3 \times 621 = $ _____   k) $5 \times 411 = $ _____   l) $2 \times 444 = $ _____

m) $3 \times 632 = $ _____   n) $4 \times 422 = $ _____   o) $4 \times 212 = $ _____   p) $2 \times 421 = $ _____

4. a) Stacy placed 821 books in each of 4 bookshelves. How many books did she place altogether?

   b) David put 723 pencils in each of 3 boxes. How many pencils did he put in the boxes?

How to solve $3 \times 42 = 3 \times 40 + 3 \times 2$

$= 3 \times 4$ tens $+ 3 \times 2$ ones

Step 1:

Multiply the ones digit by 3
(3×2 ones $= 6$ ones).

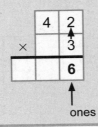

ones

Step 2:

Multiply the tens digit by 3
(3×4 tens $= 12$ tens).

Regroup 10 tens as 1 hundred.

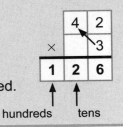

hundreds   tens

5. Use **Steps 1** and **2** to find the product.

a)

	9	4
×		2

b)

	8	3
×		3

c)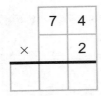

	7	4
×		2

d)

	6	3
×		2

e)

	9	2
×		3

How to solve $7 \times 53 = 7 \times 50 + 7 \times 3$

$= 7 \times 5$ tens $+ 7 \times 3$ ones

Step 1:

Multiply 3 ones by 7
($7 \times 3 = 21$).

Step 2:

Regroup 20 ones as 2 tens.

6. Complete **Steps 1** and **2** of the multiplication.

a)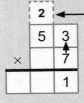

	3	
	2	7
×		5
		5

b)

	1	5
×		6

c)

	2	5
×		3

d)

	1	6
×		3

e)

	4	9
×		5

f)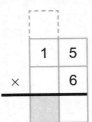

	3	6
×		4

g)

	4	7
×		2

h)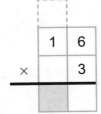

	5	8
×		3

i)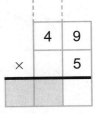

	4	7
×		6

j)

	9	7
×		8

Step 3:

Multiply 5 tens by 7
(7×5 tens = 35 tens).

Step 4:

Add 2 tens to the result
($35 + 2 = 37$ tens).

7. Complete **Steps 3** and **4** of the multiplication.

a)
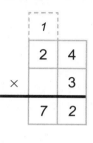

	2	4
×		3
	7	2

b)

	3	5
×		9
		5

c)

	1	5
×		5
		5

d)

	7	3
×		5
		5

e)

	8	9
×		5
		5

8. Complete **all steps** of the multiplication.

a)

	3	5
×		9

b)

	3	5
×		6

c)

	1	5
×		7

d)

	2	5
×		8

e)

	2	4
×		5

9. Multiply by regrouping ones as tens.

a)

2	2	7
×		3

b)

1	1	6
×		5

c)

2	2	4
×		3

d)

1	1	9
×		5

e)

3	2	8
×		3

10. Multiply by regrouping when you need to.

a)

2	3	7
×		5

b)

7	5	6
×		3

c)

5	2	8
×		2

d)

5	3	2
×		7

e)

2	1	3
×		8

11. A dog is 13 years old. Multiply that by 7 to estimate the dog's age in human years.

12. Anna borrowed a library book for 21 days. She reads 9 pages each day. If the book is 165 pages long, will she need to renew the book?

3. Introduction to Ratios

A **ratio** is a comparison of two quantities.

1. ☆ ◖ ○ □ ○ ○ ○ □ ☆ △ ○ ☆ ○ ◖ □

    a) The ratio of moons to circles is __2__ : __6__

    b) The ratio of triangles to moons is ____ : ____

    c) The ratio of stars to squares is ____ : ____

    d) The ratio of squares to circles is ____ : ____

    e) The ratio of squares to moons is ____ : ____

    f) The ratio of squares to figures is ____ : ____

2. Write the number of vowels compared to the number of consonants in the following words.

    a) apple   __2__ : __3__

    b) banana   ____ : ____

    c) orange   ____ : ____

    d) pear   ____ : ____

3. Write the ratio of the lengths.

    ```
    |   3   |  2  |    6    |       6      |    4   |1|    5    |
    A       B     C         D              E       F G        H
    ```

    a) *AB* to *DE* ____ : ____

    b) *BC* to *CD* ____ : ____

    c) *EF* to *FG* ____ : ____

    d) *EF* to *BC* ____ : ____

    e) *AB* to *GH* ____ : ____

    BONUS ▶ *AB* to *EG* ____ : ____

4. To make fruit salad, you need 4 cups of apples, 2 cups of oranges, and 3 cups of bananas.

    a) How many cups do you need in total? _____

    b) What is the ratio of cups of apples to cups of fruit salad? ____ : ____

5. □ ○ ○ △ □ ○ △ □ □ □

    a) In the above pattern, what does the ratio 2 : 3 describe?

    _____

    b) What does the ratio 5 : 10 describe?

    _____

6. Build a model or draw a picture that could be described by the ratio 3 : 4.

4. Introduction to Ratio Tables

1. Each column was made by skip counting by a number. Complete each column.

a)

4
8
12

b)

5
10

c)

3
9

d)

2
8

e)

7
21

f)

12
24

Michael makes orange paint by mixing 1 cup of red paint for every 3 cups of yellow paint. He records the number of cups in a **ratio table**.

In a ratio table, you must multiply the numbers in the **first row** by the same number to get another row.

Cups of Red	Cups of Yellow
1	3
2	6
3	9
4	12

×2 ×3 ×4

×2 ×3 ×4

2. Use skip counting or multiplication to complete a ratio table for each ratio.

a) 4 : 1

4	1
8	2
12	3
16	4

b) 1 : 2

1	2
2	4

c) 3 : 1

3	1

d) 1 : 7

1	7

e) 2 : 3

2	3

f) 5 : 2

5	2

g) 6 : 4

6	4

h) 3 : 5

3	5

3. Find the missing number(s) in each ratio table.

a) 2 : 7

2	7
4	14
6	

b) 4 : 1

4	1
8	2
	3

c) 3 : 2

3	2
	4
9	

BONUS ▶ 6 : _____

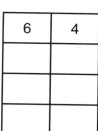

6	
12	10
18	15

4. Jackie created an increasing pattern with squares and recorded the number of squares in a table.

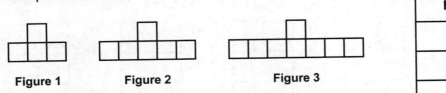

Figure 1   Figure 2   Figure 3

Figure	# of Squares
1	4
2	6
3	8

Is this a ratio table? _____ Explain how you know. _____

_____

_____

5. Circle the table(s) that is/are a ratio table.

7	3
14	6
21	9
28	12

4	2
8	5
12	8
16	11

6	5
12	10
18	15
24	20

1	5
2	6
3	7
4	8

6. Don makes punch. He needs 5 cups of ginger ale for every 3 cups of cranberry juice. Use the following ratio table to find out how many cups of ginger ale he needs for 9 cups of cranberry juice.

Cups of Ginger Ale	Cups of Cranberry Juice
5	3

BONUS ▶ In Question 6, how many cups each of ginger ale and cranberry juice does Don need to make 40 cups of punch? Use the following ratio table to find out.

Cups of Ginger Ale	Cups of Cranberry Juice	Cups in Total
5	3	8

5. Unit Rates

In a **unit rate**, one quantity is equal to 1.

For example, "30¢ for each apple" is a unit rate.

1. Complete the table for each rate.

   a) Each ticket costs $4.

# of Tickets	Cost ($)
1	4
2	8
3	12

   b) 3 hours of practice every day

Time (h)	# of Days
3	1
6	2

   c) 25 students in each class

# of Students	# of Classes

   d) Each girl has 5 flowers.

# of Girls	# of Flowers

   e) 60 miles every hour

Time (h)	Distance (mi)
1	60

   f) 6 cards for each boy

# of Cards	# of Boys

2. A blue whale typically travels 12 miles every hour. Use the following table
   to find out how long it takes for a blue whale to travel 48 miles.

Distance (mi)	Time (h)
12	1

   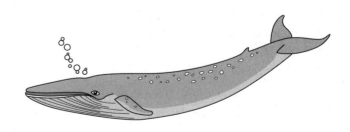

3. Multiply to find the missing information.

   a)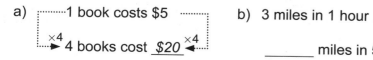
   1 book costs $5
   ×4 → 4 books cost _$20_ ×4 ←

   b) 3 miles in 1 hour

   _____ miles in 5 hours

   c) 1 teacher for 25 students

   3 teachers for _____ .

4. Measure the height of each picture. Then find the height of each animal in real life if 1 cm in the picture represents 50 cm in real life.

a) Height of picture _____ cm

Height of animal _____ cm

b) Height of picture _____ cm

Height of animal _____ cm

c) Height of picture _____ cm

Height of animal _____ cm

5. Find the missing information.

a) $15 allowance in 1 week

_____ allowance in 4 weeks

b) 60 miles in 1 hour

_____ miles in 5 hours

6. David earns $11 per hour for mowing lawns. How much will he earn in 6 hours?

7. The fuel economy of a car (how far it can go with a unit of gas) is reported in miles per gallon (MPG). Car A has a fuel economy of 30 MPG and Car B has a fuel economy of 40 MPG.

a) Complete the tables to find out which car uses less gas for a 120-mile trip.

Car A

Gas Used (gal)	Distance (mi)
1	30

Car B

Gas Used (gal)	Distance (mi)
1	40

b) Suppose gas costs $4 for every gallon. How much will the gas for the trip cost?

For Car A: _____

For Car B: _____

c) Which car has a better fuel economy? _____ Explain how you know. _____

6. Finding Unit Rates

1. Divide to find the missing information.

a) ┄┄ 6 mangoes cost $18

     ÷6
     ➤ 1 mango costs _____

b) 4 cakes cost $16

     1 cake costs _____

c) 5 pears cost $20

     1 pear costs _____

d) 3 notebooks cost $24

     1 notebook costs _____

e) 2 jackets cost $20

     1 jacket costs _____

BONUS ▶ 150 miles per 5 gallons

     _____ miles per 1 gallon

John paid $10 for 5 hot dogs. He wants to know how much 1 hot dog costs.

Step 1: He makes a chart showing the cost for each quantity of hot dogs.

He writes a question mark (?) for the missing quantity.

Step 2: He finds the number being divided by in the first column.

Then he divides by that number in the second column to find the missing number.

John finds that 1 hot dog costs $2.

Hot Dogs	Costs ($)
5	10
1	?

Hot Dogs	Costs ($)
5	10
1	2

÷5   ÷5

---

2. a) Ron earns $66 babysitting for 6 hours.

     How much does he earn in an hour?

b) Tina earns $75 cutting lawns for 5 hours.

     How much does she earn in an hour?

3. Find the unit rate.

a) 4 kg of rice for 24 cups of water

     1 kg of rice for _____ cups of water

b) 36 miles in 3 hours

     _____ miles in 1 hour

4. Find the unit rate from each table.

# of Tickets	Cost ($)
3	15
4	20
5	25

Time (h)	Distance (mi)
2	50
3	75
4	100

# of Buses	# of Students
2	40
4	80
8	160

a) $5 for each ticket

b) ☐ miles every hour

c) ☐ students in each bus

7. Integers

The height above sea level and the depth below
sea level are recorded on a scale that includes zero (0),
positive whole numbers (1, 2, 3, …), and
negative whole numbers (−1, −2, −3, …).

These numbers are called **integers**.

2 — 2 m above sea level

1 — 1 m above sea level

0 — sea level

−1 — 1 m below sea level

−2 — 2 m below sea level

1. a) Write an integer for the level at which each animal typically flies or swims.

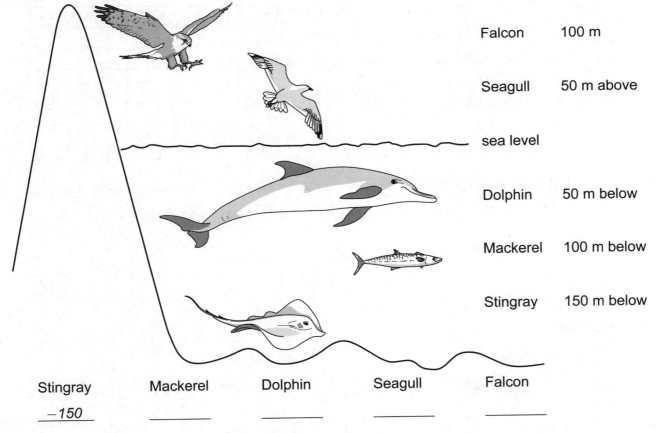

Falcon	100 m
Seagull	50 m above
sea level	
Dolphin	50 m below
Mackerel	100 m below
Stingray	150 m below

Stingray   Mackerel   Dolphin   Seagull   Falcon

−150   _____   _____   _____   _____

b) Which animal swims above the other, the dolphin or the mackerel? _____

One integer is **greater than** another if it is

• higher up on a vertical number line or
• further right on a horizontal number line.

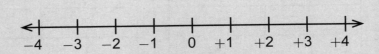

The inequality sign > means "is greater than" and < means "is less than."

c) Write an integer inequality to show your answer in part b): _____ < _____

JUMP Math Accumula

Integers that are **greater than 0** are called **positive integers**. Integers that are **less than 0** are called **negative integers**.

Positive integers are sometimes written with a "+" sign in front. Example: 3 can be written as 3 or +3, but −3 is only written as −3.

2. Label the following numbers on the number line with their letters.

   E. 6   **O.** −3   **G.** −7   **L.** −5   **B.** 3

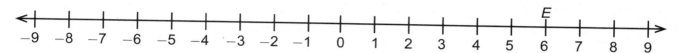

3. Write the integers on the number line.

   A. −3   **B.** +3   **C.** −4   **D.** +7   **E.** −2

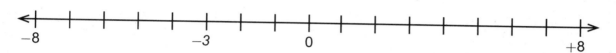

4. Circle the greater integer in each pair. Hint: Use the number line from Question 2.

   a) −3 or +5   b) +7 or −2   c) +8 or +3   d) −5 or −4

5. a) Circle the integers on the number line: 3   −4   −8   −1   7

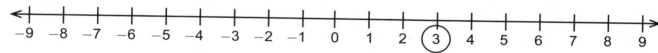

   b) Order the integers you circled from least to greatest.

   _____ < _____ < _____ < _____ < _____

6. Write < (is less than) or > (is greater than) in the box.

   a) +3 ☐ +7   b) −5 ☐ +4   c) +7 ☐ −2   d) −4 ☐ −6

7. Put the integers into the boxes in order, from greatest to least.

   +5, −3, +10, −7, −2 ⟶ ☐ > ☐ > ☐ > ☐ > ☐

8. Use any of the number lines above to answer these questions.

   a) How many negative integers are greater than (to the right of) −4? _____

   b) Write 3 integers that are less than −5. _____, _____, _____

   c) How many integers are between −4 and +2? _____

   d) Which integers are closer together, −3 and +3 or −4 and +4? _____

Temperature is also recorded using integers. Some places on Earth, and on other planets, are cold enough to have negative temperatures.

9. Write "warmer" or "colder," then write > or < to show your answer.

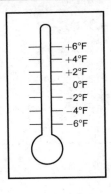

a) +3°F is _____ than −4°F, so +3 ☐ −4.

b) −5°F is _____ than −2°F, so −5 ☐ −2.

c) −3°F is _____ than −6°F, so −3 ☐ −6.

10. The graph shows the average temperature on the planets in our solar system.

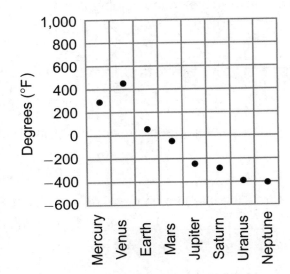

a) What is the warmest average temperature?

About _____ °F

b) What is the coldest average temperature?

About _____ °F

BONUS ▶ What is the difference between the coldest average temperature and the warmest average temperature?

About _____ °F

11. The temperature in Deadhorse, Alaska, was −8°F on Monday and −11°F on Tuesday.

Which day was warmer? _____

Integers can be used to describe quantities having opposite directions from a given point.

Examples: temperatures above (+) and below (−) zero, golf scores above (+) and below (−) par, hours ahead of (+) or behind (−) London, England.

12. Write an integer to represent each quantity.

a) A temperature of fifty-two above zero _____

b) A depth of two hundred meters below sea level _____

c) A golf score of 5 shots above par _____

d) A height of three hundred meters above sea level _____

e) 5 hours behind London, England _____

8. Models of Fractions

A **fraction** names a part of a whole.

The pie is cut into 4 equal parts.
3 parts out of 4 are shaded.

So $\frac{3}{4}$ of the pie is shaded.

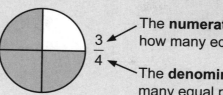

The **numerator** (3) tells you how many equal parts are shaded.

$\frac{3}{4}$

The **denominator** (4) tells you how many equal parts are in a whole.

1. Name the fraction.

   a)   b)   c)   d)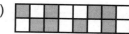

2. Use a centimeter ruler to divide the box into equal parts.

   a) 3 equal parts

   b) 10 equal parts

3. Using a centimeter ruler, find what fraction of the box is shaded.

   a)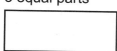

   is shaded.

   b)

   is shaded.

4. Using a centimeter ruler, complete the figure to make a whole.

   a) 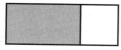 b) 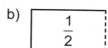 c)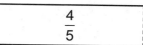

5. You have $\frac{5}{8}$ of a pie.

   a) What does the denominator (bottom) of the fraction tell you?

   b) What does the numerator (top) of the fraction tell you?

6. Which pictures show $\frac{1}{4}$ and which do not show $\frac{1}{4}$? Explain.

   a)   b)   c) 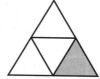 d)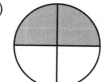

Fractions can name parts of a set: $\frac{1}{5}$ of the figures are squares, $\frac{1}{5}$ are circles, and $\frac{3}{5}$ are pentagons.

7. Fill in the blank.

a) _____ of the figures are circles.

b) _____ of the figures are white.

c) _____ of the figures are white circles.

d) _____ of the figures are shaded pentagons.

e) $\frac{4}{7}$ of the figures are _____.

f) $\frac{5}{7}$ of the figures are _____.

BONUS ▶ $\frac{0}{7}$ of the figures are _____.

8. Describe this set in two different ways using the fraction $\frac{3}{5}$.

a) $\frac{3}{5}$ of the figures are _____.

b) $\frac{3}{5}$ of the figures are _____.

9. A hockey team wins 6 games, loses 4 games, and ties one game.

What fraction of the games did the team …

a) win?

b) lose?

c) tie?

10. A box contains 2 blue marbles, 3 red marbles, and 4 yellow marbles.

What fraction of the marbles are *not* blue?

11. There are 23 children in a class. Each child chose to do a science project on animals or on plants.

The chart shows the number who chose each topic.

a) Fill in the missing numbers in the chart.

b) What fraction of the children chose to study animals?

c) What fraction of the girls chose to study plants?

	Animals	Plants
Boys	7	4
Girls		
Children	12	

12. What fraction of the squares are on the outside of the figure?

9. Mixed Numbers and Improper Fractions

Mattias and his friends ate the amount of pie shown.

They ate two and three quarter pies

altogether (or $2\frac{3}{4}$ pies).

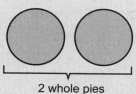

2 whole pies   and $\frac{3}{4}$ of another pie

$2\frac{3}{4}$ is called a **mixed number** because it is a mixture of a whole number and a fraction.

1. Find the mixed number for each picture.

a)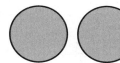

___2___ whole pies and $\frac{1}{3}$

of another pie = $2\frac{1}{3}$ pies

b)

_____ whole pie and

of another pie = _____ pies

c)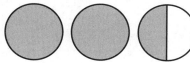

_____ whole pies and

of another pie = _____ pies

2. Find the mixed number for each picture.

a)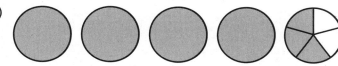

b)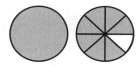

c)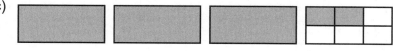

d)

3. Shade the area given by the mixed number. Note: There may be more figures than you need.

a) $2\frac{1}{3}$

b) $3\frac{1}{4}$

c) $1\frac{5}{6}$

d) $2\frac{4}{5}$

4. Sketch.

a) $3\frac{3}{4}$ pies

b) $2\frac{1}{3}$ pies

c) $2\frac{5}{6}$ pies

d) $3\frac{7}{8}$ pies

5. Which fraction represents more pie: $3\frac{2}{3}$, $4\frac{1}{4}$, or $4\frac{3}{4}$? How do you know?

6. Is $5\frac{3}{4}$ closer to 5 or 6?

Huan-Yue and her friends ate 9 quarter-sized pieces of pizza.

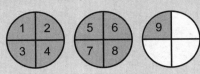

$$\frac{9}{4} = 2\frac{1}{4}$$

improper fraction   mixed number

Altogether, they ate $\frac{9}{4}$ pizzas.

When the numerator of a fraction is greater than the denominator, the fraction represents **more than a whole**. Such fractions are called **improper fractions**.

7. Write the fraction as an improper fraction.

a)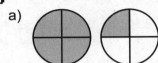

b)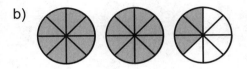

c)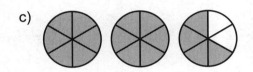

d)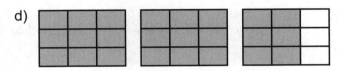

e)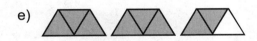

f)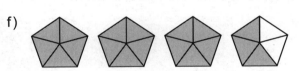

8. Shade one piece at a time until you have shaded the amount of pie given by the improper fraction.

a) $\frac{7}{2}$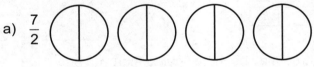

b) $\frac{9}{4}$

c) $\frac{8}{3}$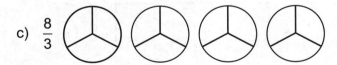

d) $\frac{15}{5}$

9. Sketch.

a) $\frac{13}{4}$ pies   b) $\frac{7}{3}$ pies   c) $\frac{9}{2}$ pies   d) $\frac{11}{6}$ pies

10. Which fraction represents more pie: $\frac{7}{4}$, $\frac{9}{4}$, or $\frac{9}{3}$? Justify your answer with a picture.

11. Is the fraction an improper fraction? How do you know?

a) $\frac{5}{7}$ b) $\frac{9}{8}$ c) $\frac{13}{11}$ d) $\frac{11}{13}$

12. Find the mixed number for each picture.

a)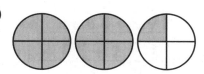

   __2__ whole pies and

   $\dfrac{1}{4}$ of another pie

   $= 2\dfrac{1}{4}$ pies

b)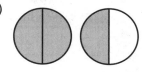

   ____ whole pies and

   of another pie

   =   pies

c)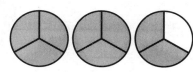

   ____ whole pies and

   of another pie

   =   pies

13. Write the fraction as a mixed number and as an improper fraction.

a)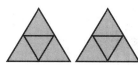

   =

b)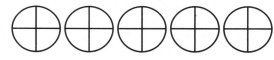

   =

14. Shade the amount of pie given by the mixed number. Then write an improper fraction for the amount.

a) $3\dfrac{1}{2}$

Improper fraction:

b) $4\dfrac{3}{4}$

Improper fraction:

15. Shade the area given by the improper fraction. Then write a mixed number for the shaded area.

a) $\dfrac{7}{3}$

Mixed number:

b) $\dfrac{17}{6}$

Mixed number:

c) $\dfrac{13}{5}$

Mixed number:

d) $\dfrac{21}{8}$

Mixed number:

16. Draw a picture to find out which number is greater.

a) $3\dfrac{1}{2}$ or $\dfrac{5}{3}$

b) $1\dfrac{4}{5}$ or $\dfrac{11}{5}$

c) $\dfrac{15}{8}$ or $\dfrac{7}{3}$

d) $\dfrac{13}{4}$ or $2\dfrac{2}{3}$

17. How could you use division to find out how many whole pies are in $\dfrac{13}{5}$ of a pie? Explain.

10. More Mixed Numbers and Improper Fractions

How many quarter pieces are in $2\frac{3}{4}$ pies?

There are 4 quarter pieces in 1 pie.

So there are 11 quarter pieces altogether.

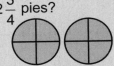

There are 2 × 4 quarters in 2 pies.

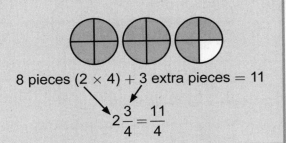

8 pieces (2 × 4) + 3 extra pieces = 11

$$2\frac{3}{4} = \frac{11}{4}$$

1. Find the number of **halves** in each amount.

   a) 1 pie = _____ halves

   b) 2 pies = _____ halves

   c) 4 pies = _____ halves

   d) $3\frac{1}{2}$ pies = _____ halves

   e) $4\frac{1}{2}$ pies = _____ halves

   f) $5\frac{1}{2}$ pies = _____

2. Each pie has 3 pieces, so each piece is a third. Find the number of **thirds** in each amount.

   a) 1 pie = ___3___ thirds

   b) 2 pies = _____ thirds

   c) 4 pies = _____ thirds

   d) $1\frac{1}{3}$ pies = _____ thirds

   e) $2\frac{2}{3}$ pies = _____

   f) $5\frac{2}{3}$ pies = _____

3. A box holds 4 cans, so each can is a fourth. Find the number of cans each amount holds.

   a) 2 boxes hold _____ cans.

   b) $2\frac{1}{4}$ boxes hold _____ cans.

   c) $3\frac{3}{4}$ boxes hold _____ cans.

   d) $2\frac{3}{4}$ boxes hold _____ cans.

4. If a bag holds 12 peas, then …

   a) $1\frac{1}{12}$ bags hold _____ peas.

   b) $2\frac{7}{12}$ bags hold _____ peas.

5. Write the mixed numbers as improper fractions.

   a) $2\frac{1}{3} = \frac{}{3}$

   b) $5\frac{1}{2} = \frac{}{2}$

   c) $4\frac{2}{5} = \frac{}{5}$

   d) $7\frac{1}{4} = \frac{}{4}$

6. Envelopes come in packs of 6. Alice used $2\frac{5}{6}$ packs. How many envelopes did she use? _____

7. Maia and her friends ate $4\frac{3}{4}$ pizzas. How many quarter-sized pieces did they eat? _____

BONUS ▶ How many quarters are in $4\frac{1}{2}$ dollars? _____

Win-Chi has 13 party gifts to give out at his birthday party. He packs 3 gifts in each bag.

Win-Chi can give out 4 bags, but there is one party gift left over. The leftover gift is called the **remainder**.

13 ÷ 3 = 4 Remainder 1 OR **13 ÷ 3 = 4 R 1**

"R" means "Remainder"

8. Can 9 party gifts all be packed into bags of 2? Show your work with a picture.

9. Put as many gifts as you can into bags. Show your work with a picture.

a) 11 gifts altogether; 3 gifts in each bag

b) 17 gifts altogether; 4 gifts in each bag

_____ bags; _____ gifts remaining

_____ bags; _____ gifts remaining

10. Put as many dots as you can into circles. Draw a picture and write a division equation.

a) 2 dots in each circle; 11 dots altogether

b) 5 dots in each circle; 23 dots altogether

__11__ ÷ __2__ = _____ R _____

_____ ÷ _____ = _____ R _____

11. How many whole pies are there and how many leftover pieces?
Draw a picture and write a division equation to show your answer.

a) Pies are each cut into four pieces. There are 14 pieces of pie in total.

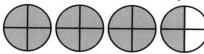

14 ÷ 4 = _____ R _____
$\quad\quad\quad\quad$ whole pies $\quad$ leftover pieces

b) Pies are each cut into six pieces. There are 17 pieces of pie altogether.

How many whole pies are in $\frac{13}{4}$ pies?

There are 13 pieces altogether, and each pie has 4 pieces: **13 ÷ 4 = 3 Remainder 1**

There are 3 whole pies and 1 quarter left over: 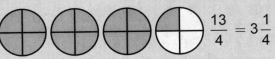 $\frac{13}{4} = 3\frac{1}{4}$

12. Find the number of whole pies in each amount by dividing.

a) $\frac{4}{2}$ pies = _____ whole pies

b) $\frac{15}{3}$ pies = _____ whole pies

c) $\frac{8}{4}$ pies = _____ whole pies

13. Find the number of whole pies and the number of pieces remaining by dividing.

a) $\frac{5}{2}$ pies = ___2___ whole pies and ___1___ half pie = $2\frac{1}{2}$ pies

b) $\frac{9}{2}$ pies = _____ whole pies and _____ half pie = _____ pies

c) $\frac{10}{3}$ pies

d) $\frac{15}{4}$ pies

e) $\frac{18}{5}$ pies

f) $\frac{17}{9}$ pies

BONUS ▶ $\frac{70}{9}$ pies

14. Divide the numerator by the denominator to write each improper fraction as a mixed number.

a) $\frac{13}{3}$ 13 ÷ 3 = _4_ R _1_

So $\frac{13}{3} = 4\frac{1}{3}$

b) $\frac{13}{6}$ 13 ÷ 6 = ___ R ___

So $\frac{13}{6}$ =

c) $\frac{15}{4}$ 15 ÷ 4 = ___ R ___

So $\frac{15}{4}$ =

d) $\frac{3}{2}$ =

e) $\frac{8}{3}$ =

f) $\frac{22}{5}$ =

15. Write a mixed number and an improper fraction for the total number of liters.

1 L

16. Write a mixed number and an improper fraction for the length of the rope.

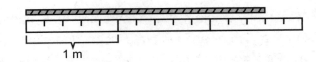

1 m

Since $\frac{7}{4} = 1\frac{3}{4}$, their opposites are equal too: $-\frac{7}{4} = -1\frac{3}{4}$.

17. Complete the chart.

Mixed Number	$-2\frac{3}{4}$	$-3\frac{2}{5}$		$-4\frac{1}{2}$				$-1\frac{3}{8}$
Improper Fraction	$-\frac{11}{4}$		$-\frac{7}{5}$		$-\frac{8}{3}$	$-\frac{9}{4}$	$-\frac{11}{3}$	

JUMP Math Accumula

11. Equivalent Fractions

Two or more fractions are **equivalent** if they can be shown by the same part of the same whole.

Example: $\frac{2}{3}$ and $\frac{4}{6}$ are equivalent fractions.

$\frac{2}{3} =$ 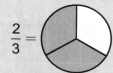 $\frac{4}{6} =$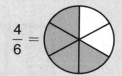

1. What equivalent fractions do these pictures show?

$\frac{1}{2}$ = _____ = _____ = _____

2. Shade the same part to find a fraction equivalent to the first fraction.

a)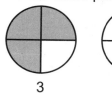

$\frac{3}{4}$ = _____

b)

$\frac{1}{3}$ = _____

c)

$\frac{3}{5}$ = _____

d)

$\frac{4}{5}$ = _____

3. How many times as many parts?

a) has _____ times as many parts as

b) has _____ times as many parts as

c) has _____ times as many parts as

4. Fill in the blanks.

a) A has _____ times as many parts as B.

    A has _____ times as many shaded parts as B.

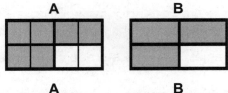

b) A has _____ times as many parts as B.

    A has _____ times as many shaded parts as B.

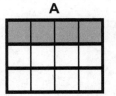

c) A has _____ times as many parts as B.

    A has _____ times as many shaded parts as B.

5. The picture shows two equivalent fractions. How many times as much as the first numerator and denominator are the second numerator and denominator?

a) 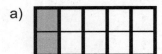 $\dfrac{1}{5}$ and $\dfrac{2}{10}$

b) 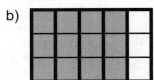 $\dfrac{4}{5}$ and $\dfrac{12}{15}$

2 is _____ times as much as 1.

10 is _____ times as much as 5.

12 is _____ times as much as 4.

15 is _____ times as much as 5.

6. Write another equivalent fraction for each picture. Then write how many times as much as the first numerator and denominator the second numerator and denominator are.

a)  $\dfrac{3}{4} = \boxed{\dfrac{9}{12}}$

b) 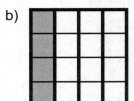 $\dfrac{1}{4} = \boxed{}$

_____ times as much

_____ times as much

c) 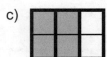 $\dfrac{2}{3} = \boxed{}$

BONUS ▶

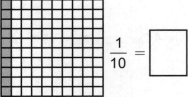 $\dfrac{1}{10} = \boxed{}$

_____ times as much

_____ times as much

You can multiply the numerator and denominator by the same number to get an equivalent fraction.

Example: Picture A   Picture B

$$\frac{3}{4} \xrightarrow[\times 2]{\times 2} \frac{6}{8}$$

Picture B has twice as many **parts** as Picture A.
Picture B has twice as many **shaded parts** as Picture A.

7. Draw lines to cut the pies into more pieces. Then fill in the numerators of the equivalent fractions.

a)

4 pieces   6 pieces   8 pieces

$$\frac{1}{2} = \frac{}{4} = \frac{}{6} = \frac{}{8}$$

b)

6 pieces   9 pieces   12 pieces

$$\frac{1}{3} = \frac{}{6} = \frac{}{9} = \frac{}{12}$$

8. Cut each pie into more pieces. Then fill in the missing numbers.

a) $\frac{2}{3} \xrightarrow[\times 2]{\times 2} \frac{}{6}$

↑ This number tells you how many pieces to cut each slice into.

b) 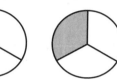 $\frac{3}{4} \xrightarrow[\times 2]{\times 2} \frac{}{8}$

c) $\frac{2}{3} \xrightarrow[\times]{\times} \frac{}{9}$

9. Use multiplication to find the equivalent fraction.

a) $\frac{1 \times 2}{3 \times 2} = \frac{}{6}$

b) $\frac{1 \times}{2 \times} = \frac{}{10}$

c) $\frac{2}{5} = \frac{}{10}$

d) $\frac{3}{4} = \frac{}{8}$

e) $\frac{1}{4} = \frac{}{12}$

f) $\frac{4}{5} = \frac{}{15}$

g) $\frac{5}{6} = \frac{}{12}$

h) $\frac{3}{10} = \frac{}{100}$

i) $\frac{5}{9} = \frac{}{72}$

10. Write five fractions equivalent to $\frac{7}{10}$.

$$\frac{7}{10} = \boxed{} = \boxed{} = \boxed{} = \boxed{} = \boxed{}$$

12. Lowest Common Multiples (LCMs)

The **whole numbers** are the numbers 0, 1, 2, 3, and so on. The **multiples** of a whole number are the numbers you get by multiplying the number by another whole number.

Examples:

The multiples of 2 are $2 \times 0 = \mathbf{0}$ $2 \times 1 = \mathbf{2}$ $2 \times 2 = \mathbf{4}$ $2 \times 3 = \mathbf{6}$ $2 \times 4 = \mathbf{8}$ ...

The multiples of 3 are $3 \times 0 = \mathbf{0}$ $3 \times 1 = \mathbf{3}$ $3 \times 2 = \mathbf{6}$ $3 \times 3 = \mathbf{9}$ $3 \times 4 = \mathbf{12}$ ...

1. a) Skip count to write the multiples of 3 up to 3×10.

   __0__ , __3__ , _____ , _____ , _____ , _____ , _____ , _____ , _____ , _____ , _____

   b) Use your answers in part a) to circle the multiples of 3.

   12   17   22   24   25   27

A number is a **common multiple** of two numbers if it is a multiple of both of them.

2. Mark the multiples of the two numbers on the number lines. Then write their common multiples.

   a) Which numbers are common multiples of both 3 and 4?

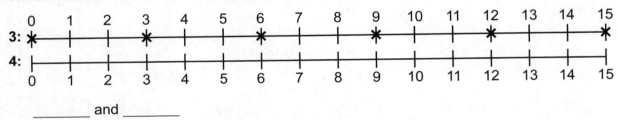

   _____ and _____

   b) Which numbers are common multiples of both 2 and 3?

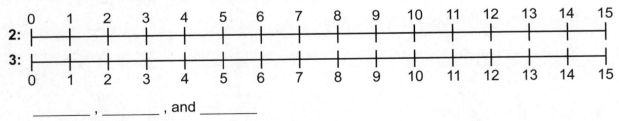

   _____ , _____ , and _____

   c) Which numbers are common multiples of both 4 and 6?

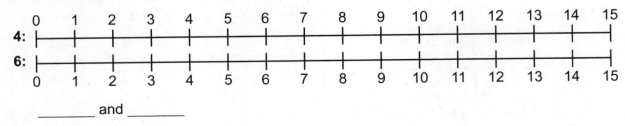

   _____ and _____

3. List the multiples of both numbers, up to 10 times each number.

Write the first two common multiples, not including 0.

a) 3 and 4

3: _0, 3, 6, 9, 12, 15, 18, 21, 24, 27, 30_

4: _____

The first two common multiples are _____ and _____.

b) 2 and 3

2: _____

3: _____

The first two common multiples are _____ and _____.

c) 3 and 5   d) 2 and 5   e) 2 and 4   f) 4 and 5

The number 0 is a multiple of every number. The **lowest common multiple (LCM)** of two numbers is the smallest whole number (not 0) that is a multiple of both numbers.

4. Find the lowest common multiple of each pair of numbers.

a) 4 and 10

4: _4, 8, 12, 16, 20_

10: _10, 20_

LCM = _____

b) 3 and 6

3:

6:

LCM = _____

c) 4 and 6

4:

6:

LCM = _____

d) 5 and 10

5:

10:

LCM = _____

e) 6 and 8

6:

8:

LCM = _____

f) 5 and 7

5:

7:

LCM = _____

g) 8 and 10   h) 8 and 12   i) 8 and 16

5. Find the LCM of each number and itself.

a) 3 and 3 _____   b) 4 and 4 _____   c) 5 and 5 _____

BONUS ▶ The LCM of 183 and 183 is _____.

To find the lowest common multiple of two numbers, write the first few multiples of the *larger* number until you see one that is also a multiple of the smaller number:

Example: Find the LCM of 3 and 5.

The first few multiples of 5 are 5, 10, 15. ⟵—— Stop here because 15 is a multiple of 3.

6. Find the lowest common multiple.

a) 6 and 10

10, 20, 30

LCM = ___30___

b) 9 and 12

LCM = _____

c) 7 and 10

LCM = _____

d) 6 and 9

LCM = _____

e) 6 and 15

LCM = _____

f) 8 and 9

LCM = _____

g) 5 and 8

LCM = _____

h) 3 and 6

LCM = _____

7. a) Write the LCM of each pair of numbers.

i) 2 and 3 _____   ii) 2 and 4 _____   iii) 2 and 5 _____   iv) 2 and 6 _____

v) 2 and 7 _____   vi) 2 and 8 _____   vii) 2 and 9 _____   viii) 2 and 10 _____

b) For which numbers in part a) is the LCM of 2 and the number equal to the number itself?

_____ , _____ , _____ , and _____

c) What is the LCM of 2 and 184? How do you know? _____

_____

13. Applying LCMs and GCFs to Fractions

1. Imagine moving the shaded pieces from pies A and B onto pie plate C.
   Show how much of C would be filled, then write a fraction for C.

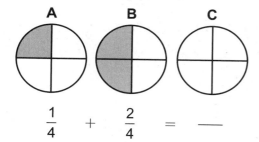

$$\frac{1}{4} + \frac{2}{4} = \underline{\quad}$$

2. Imagine pouring the liquid from cups A and B into C. Shade the amount of liquid
   that would be in C. Then complete the addition equations.

a)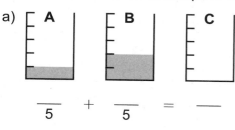

$$\frac{\quad}{5} + \frac{\quad}{5} = \underline{\quad}$$

b)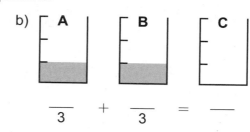

$$\frac{\quad}{3} + \frac{\quad}{3} = \underline{\quad}$$

3. Add.

a) $\dfrac{3}{5} + \dfrac{1}{5} =$ b) $\dfrac{2}{4} + \dfrac{1}{4} =$ c) $\dfrac{3}{7} + \dfrac{2}{7} =$ d) $\dfrac{5}{8} + \dfrac{2}{8} =$

e) $\dfrac{3}{11} + \dfrac{7}{11} =$ f) $\dfrac{5}{17} + \dfrac{9}{17} =$ g) $\dfrac{11}{24} + \dfrac{10}{24} =$ h) $\dfrac{3}{57} + \dfrac{13}{57} =$

4. Show how much pie would be left if you took away the amount shown.
   Then complete the fraction statement.

a)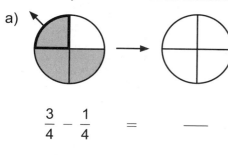

$$\frac{3}{4} - \frac{1}{4} = \underline{\quad}$$

b)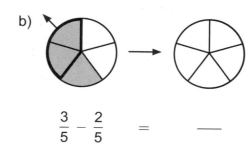

$$\frac{3}{5} - \frac{2}{5} = \underline{\quad}$$

5. Subtract.

a) $\dfrac{2}{3} - \dfrac{1}{3} =$ b) $\dfrac{3}{5} - \dfrac{1}{5} =$ c) $\dfrac{6}{7} - \dfrac{3}{7} =$ d) $\dfrac{5}{8} - \dfrac{2}{8} =$

e) $\dfrac{9}{12} - \dfrac{2}{12} =$ f) $\dfrac{6}{19} - \dfrac{4}{19} =$ g) $\dfrac{9}{28} - \dfrac{3}{28} =$ h) $\dfrac{17}{57} - \dfrac{12}{57} =$

Follow the steps to add or subtract fractions with different denominators.

Example: $\dfrac{1}{3} + \dfrac{2}{5}$

Step 1: Find the **lowest common denominator (LCD)** of the fractions (the LCM of the denominators).
Example: The LCM of the denominators, 3 and 5, is 15.

Step 2: Create equivalent fractions with that denominator.
Example: $\dfrac{1}{3} + \dfrac{2}{5} = \dfrac{5 \times 1}{5 \times 3} + \dfrac{2 \times 3}{5 \times 3} = \dfrac{5}{15} + \dfrac{6}{15} = \dfrac{11}{15}$

6. Find the LCD of each pair of fractions. Then show what numbers you would multiply the numerator and denominator of each fraction by in order to add.

a) $\dfrac{3 \times 1}{3 \times 2} + \dfrac{2 \times 2}{3 \times 2}$

LCD = ___6___

b) $\dfrac{3}{4} + \dfrac{1}{8}$

LCD = _____

c) $\dfrac{1}{6} + \dfrac{2}{9}$

LCD = _____

d) $\dfrac{1}{4} + \dfrac{2}{3}$

LCD = _____

e) $\dfrac{1}{4} + \dfrac{1}{6}$

LCD = _____

f) $\dfrac{2}{5} + \dfrac{1}{10}$

LCD = _____

7. Add or subtract the fractions by changing them to equivalent fractions with denominators equal to the LCD of the fractions.

a) $\dfrac{2}{5} + \dfrac{1}{4}$

=

=

b) $\dfrac{4}{15} + \dfrac{2}{3}$

=

=

c) $\dfrac{5}{6} + \dfrac{3}{8}$

=

=

d) $\dfrac{1}{6} + \dfrac{11}{24}$

e) $\dfrac{5}{28} - \dfrac{1}{7}$

f) $\dfrac{4}{9} - \dfrac{1}{6}$

g) $\dfrac{3}{8} + \dfrac{7}{16}$

h) $\dfrac{7}{16} - \dfrac{3}{8}$

i) $\dfrac{7}{9} - \dfrac{3}{8}$

BONUS ▶ $\dfrac{4}{15} + \dfrac{1}{3} + \dfrac{2}{5}$

8. Find the GCF of each pair of numbers.

   a) 3 and 4   b) 6 and 10   c) 5 and 8   d) 6 and 9

   _____   _____   _____   _____

A fraction is reduced to **lowest terms** when the GCF of its numerator and denominator is equal to 1.

Example: $\frac{3}{4}$ is in lowest terms, but $\frac{6}{8}$ is not.

9. Find the GCF of the numerator and denominator. Then decide if the fraction is in lowest terms.

Fraction	$\frac{3}{6}$	$\frac{2}{5}$	$\frac{4}{5}$	$\frac{5}{10}$	$\frac{6}{10}$	$\frac{7}{10}$	$\frac{15}{16}$	$\frac{9}{5}$
GCF	3							
Lowest terms?	No							

10. Reduce the fractions below by dividing the numerator and the denominator by their GCF.

   a) $\frac{2 \div 2}{10 \div 2} = \frac{1}{5}$ b) $\frac{4 \div}{12 \div} =$ c) $\frac{6 \div}{9 \div} =$ d) $\frac{20 \div}{25 \div} =$

11. Add or subtract, then reduce your answer to lowest terms.

   a) $\frac{5 \times 1}{5 \times 6} + \frac{1 \times 3}{10 \times 3}$ b) $\frac{13}{15} - \frac{1}{5}$ c) $\frac{5}{6} + \frac{3}{10}$ d) $\frac{25}{28} - \frac{1}{7}$

   $= \frac{5}{30} + \frac{3}{30}$

   $= \frac{8}{30}$

   $= \frac{4}{15}$

14. Numerical Expressions

A **numerical expression** is a combination of numbers, operation signs, and sometimes brackets that represents a quantity.

Example: These numerical expressions all represent 10:

$$7 + 3 \qquad 12 - 2 \qquad 100 \div 10 \qquad (4 + 1) \times 2$$

1. Calculate each numerical expression.

   a) $1 + 3 + 4$ _____

   b) 3×4 _____

   c) $2 \times 2 \times 2$ _____

   d) $(1 + 3) \times 4$ _____

   e) $3 + (4 \div 2)$ _____

   f) $(4 \times 3) \div 2$ _____

An **equation** is a statement that has two equal expressions separated by an equal sign.

Example: $12 - 2 = 100 \div 10$

2. a) Circle two expressions in Question 1 that represent the same number.

   b) Write an equation using those two expressions.

   _____ = _____

3. Verify that each equation is true.

   a) $(4 + 3) \times 2 = (5 \times 3) - 1$

   $(4 + 3) \times 2$ and $(5 \times 3) - 1$
   $= 7 \times 2 \qquad\quad = 15 - 1$
   $= 14 \qquad\qquad = 14$

   b) $3 \times 4 \times 5 = 6 \times 10$

   c) $5 + 12 = (5 + 1) + (12 - 1)$

   d) $5 + 12 = (5 + 2) + (12 - 2)$

BONUS ▶ Add brackets where necessary to the equation to make it true.

   a) $6 - 2 \times 2 = 8$

   b) $6 - 2 \times 2 = 2$

   c) $5 \times 4 - 3 = 5$

   d) $16 \div 2 \times 2 = 4$

   e) $8 - 4 \times 2 = 0$

   f) $6 \times 4 \div 2 = 12$

15. Unknown Quantities

1. Some apples are inside a box and some are outside the box. The total number of apples is shown. Draw the missing apples in the box. The first one is done for you.

a)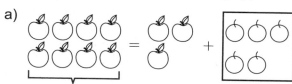

total number of apples

b)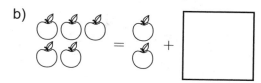

c)

total number of apples

d)

2. Draw the missing apples in the box. Then write an equation (with numbers) to represent the picture.

a)

$$\underline{\ \ 5\ \ } = \underline{\ \ 3\ \ } + \ \square$$

b)

$$\underline{\ \ \ \ \ } = \underline{\ \ \ \ \ } + \ \square$$

c)

$$\underline{\ \ \ \ \ } + \ \square = \underline{\ \ \ \ \ }$$

d)

$$\underline{\ \ \ \ \ } + \ \square = \underline{\ \ \ \ \ }$$

3. Write an equation for each situation. (Use a box for the unknown quantity.)

a) There are 9 apples altogether.

Five are outside of a box.

How many are inside?

$9 = 5 + \square$

b) There are 7 apples altogether.

Three are outside of a box.

How many are inside?

c) There are 8 pears altogether.

Three are inside a bag.

How many are outside?

d) Ten students are at the library.

Two are in the computer room.

How many are outside?

4. Tim took some apples from a box. Show how many apples were in the box originally.

a)

b)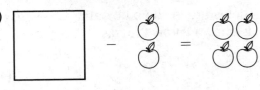

Tim took away
this many.   This is how many
were left.

c)

d)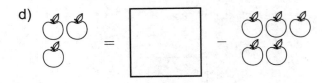

5. Show how many apples were in the box originally. Then write an equation to represent the picture.

a)

b)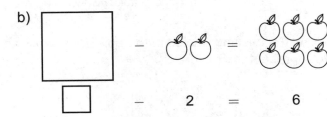

[ ] − 3 = 4

[ ] − 2 = 6

6. Find the number that makes the equation true and write it in the box.

a) [ ] + 4 = 7

b) [ ] + 3 = 6

c) [ ] + 5 = 9

d) 9 − [ ] = 6

e) 17 − [ ] = 13

f) 11 − [ ] = 9

g) 2 × [ ] = 6

h) 3 × [ ] = 15

i) 3 × [ ] = 9

j) [ ] ÷ 2 = 4

k) [ ] ÷ 5 = 3

l) [ ] ÷ 3 = 4

m) 5 + 4 = 6 + [ ]

n) 10 − 4 = [ ] + 5

o) 2 = 8 − [ ]

BONUS ▶ Put the same number in both boxes to make the equation true.

a) [ ] + 2 = 8 − [ ]

b) [ ] ÷ 2 = [ ] − 2

c) [ ] × [ ] = 9

7. Find two different answers for the equation. Put the same number in the same shapes.

△ + △ + ◯ = 5

[ ] + [ ] + ◇ = 5

16. Variables

1. Look at the sign at right, then write a numerical expression for the cost of renting skates for…

   a) 2 hours: ___3 × 2___
   b) 5 hours: _____
   c) 6 hours: _____
   d) 8 hours: _____

A **variable** is a letter or symbol (such as x, n, or H) that represents a number.

To make an **algebraic expression**, replace some numbers in a numerical expression with variables.

Examples of algebraic expressions: $x + 1$ $3 + 4 \times T$ $2 + t - 3 \times h$

---

2. Write an expression for the distance a car would travel at the given speed and time.

   a) Speed: 60 mi per hour
       Time: 2 hours
       Distance: _____ mi

   b) Speed: 80 km per hour
       Time: 3 hours
       Distance: _____ km

   c) Speed: 70 km per hour
       Time: h hours
       Distance: _____ km

In the product of a number and a variable, the multiplication sign is usually dropped.

Examples: $3 \times T$ can be written $3T$ and $5 \times z$ can be written $5z$.

---

3. Look at the sign at right, then write an algebraic expression for the cost of renting skis for…

   a) h hours: __$5 \times h$__ or __$5h$__
   b) t hours: _____ or _____
   c) x hours: _____ or _____
   d) n hours: _____ or _____

4. Write an equation that tells you the relationship between the numbers in Column A and Column B.

a)

A	B
1	4
2	5
3	6

___$A + 3 = B$___

b)

A	B
1	2
2	4
3	6

___$2 \times A = B$___
___or $2A = B$___

c)

A	B
1	3
2	4
3	5

_____

d)

A	B
1	3
2	6
3	9

_____
_____

e)

A	B
1	5
2	10
3	15

_____
_____

5. Circle the tables in Question 4 that are ratio tables.

6. Write an equation. Use the variable x for the number of apples in the box.

   a) There are 10 apples altogether.
      Four are outside of a box.

      _____

   b) There are 12 apples altogether.
      Seven are outside of a box.

      _____

When replacing a variable with a number, we use brackets.

Example: Replacing n with 7 in the expression $3n$ gives $3(7)$, which is another way to write 3×7.

---

7. Write the number 2 in the brackets and evaluate.

   a) $5(2) = \underline{5 \times 2} = \underline{10}$

   b) $3() = $ _____ = _____

   c) $4() = $ _____ = _____

   d) $2() + 5$

      $= $ _____ = _____

      $= $ _____

   e) $4() - 2$

      $= $ _____ = _____

      $= $ _____

   f) $6() + 3$

      $= $ _____ = _____

      $= $ _____

8. Replace n with 2 in each expression and evaluate.

   a) $4n + 3$

      $= 4(2) + 3$

      $= 8 + 3$

      $= 11$

   b) $5n + 1$

   c) $3n - 2$

   d) $2n + 3$

   e) $4n - 3$

   f) $2n - 4$

9. Replace the variable with the given number and evaluate.

   a) $5h + 2, \quad h = 3$

      $5(3) + 2$

      $= 15 + 2$

      $= 17$

   b) $2n + 3, \quad n = 6$

   c) $5t - 2, \quad t = 4$

   d) $3m + 9, \quad m = 8$

   e) $9 - z, \quad z = 4$

   f) $3n + 2, \quad n = 5$

10. Evaluate each expression.

    a) $2n + 3, \quad n = 5$

       $2(5) + 3$

       $= 10 + 3 = 13$

    b) $2t + 3, \quad t = 5$

    c) $2w + 3, \quad w = 5$

11. What do you notice about your answers to Question 10? _____

    Why is that so? _____

    _____

17. Modeling Equations

1. Each bag contains the same unknown number of apples. Let *x* stand for the number of apples in one bag. Write a mathematical expression for the total number of apples.

a) 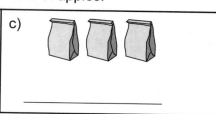	b)	c)
_____ *x* + 2 _____	_____	_____

2. Write an **expression** for the total number of apples. Write an **equation** by making the expression equal to the total number of apples.

a) There are **7 apples** in total.

Expression ___ 2*x* + 1 ___

Equation ___ 2*x* + 1 = 7 ___

b) There are **10 apples** in total.

Expression _____

Equation _____

c) There are **15 apples** in total.

Expression _____

Equation _____

3. Write an equation and find the number of apples in each bag.

a) 9 apples in total

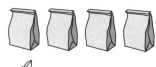

Equation ___ 4*x* + 1 = 9 ___

___2___ apples in each bag

b) 13 apples in total

Equation _____

_____ apples in each bag

c) 17 apples in total

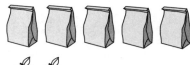

Equation _____

_____ apples in each bag

d) 11 apples in total

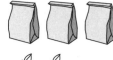

Equation _____

_____ apples in each bag

e) 14 apples in total

Equation _____

_____ apples in each bag

f) 31 apples in total

Equation _____

_____ apples in each bag

4. Does this type of model work for the equation 3*x* − 4 = 14? Explain in your notebook.

18. Solving Equations with Balances

1. The scales are balanced. Cross out the same number of apples on each side to find how many apples are in the bag.

a)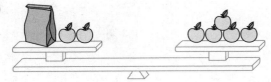

There are _____ apples in the bag.

b)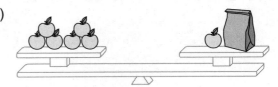

There are _____ apples in the bag.

An equation is like balanced scales. An equal sign between the sides shows that they are equal.

To solve $x + 4 = 10$, subtract 4 from both sides of the equation.

$$\begin{array}{r} x + 4 = 10 \\ -4 \quad -4 \\ \hline x = 6 \end{array}$$

2. Subtract 4 from both sides of the equation.

a) $x + 4 = 12$
$\quad -4 \quad -4$
$\quad x = \boxed{8}$

b) $x + 4 = 9$
$\quad -4 \quad -4$
$\quad x = \boxed{}$

c) $14 = x + 4$
$\quad -4 \quad -4$
$\quad \boxed{} = x$

d) $56 = x + 4$
$\quad -4 \quad -4$
$\quad \boxed{} = x$

3. Subtract the same number from both sides of the equation.

a) $x + 15 = 32$
$\quad -15 \quad -15$
$\quad x = \boxed{}$

b) $x + 43 = 59$
$\quad -43 \quad -43$
$\quad x = \boxed{}$

c) $37 = x + 19$
$\quad -19 \quad -19$
$\quad \boxed{} = x$

d) $86 = x + 38$
$\quad -38 \quad -38$
$\quad \boxed{} = x$

4. Which number will you subtract from both sides to solve the equation? Subtract the number and solve the equation.

a) $x + 5 = 12$
$\quad -\boxed{5} \quad -\boxed{}$
$\quad x = \boxed{}$

b) $x + 14 = 29$
$\quad -\boxed{} \quad -\boxed{}$
$\quad x = \boxed{}$

c) $14 = x + 8$
$\quad -\boxed{} \quad -\boxed{}$
$\quad \boxed{} = x$

d) $53 = x + 24$
$\quad -\boxed{} \quad -\boxed{}$
$\quad \boxed{} = x$

5. Solve the equation by subtracting the same number from both sides.

a) $x + 15 = 33$
$\quad -15 \quad -15$
$\quad x = 18$

b) $x + 53 = 75$

c) $44 = x + 8$

d) $42 + x = 64$

6. The scales are balanced. All bags in the same picture have the same number of apples. How many apples are in each bag?

a)

There are _____ apples in each bag.

b)

There are _____ apples in each bag.

7. Complete the picture and solve the equation. The first one is started for you.

a) $12 = 3 \times b$

$b =$ _____

b) $2 \times b = 10$

$b =$ _____

c) $4 \times b = 8$

$b =$ _____

8. Evaluate.

a) $(5 \times 3) \div 3$

= _____ $\div\ 3$

= _____

b) $(3 \times 6) \div 6$

= _____ $\div\ 6$

= _____

c) $(8 \times 7) \div 7$

= _____ $\div\ 7$

= _____

Multiplying and dividing by the same number gets you back to the number you started with.

Example: $4 \times 3 = 12$, so $12 \div 3 = 4$ or $(4 \times 3) \div 3 = 4$

You can do the same with unknown numbers and letters.

Example: $\times\ 3 =$ $\div\ 3 =$

($\blacksquare$ $\times\ 3) \div 3 =$ $\blacksquare$ or $(b \times 3) \div 3 = b$

---

9. What number will you divide the expression by to get back to b?

a) $(b \times 3) \div$ _____ $= b$

b) $(b \times 8) \div$ _____ $= b$

c) $(b \times 5) \div$ _____ $= b$

10. a) Divide both sides by the same number to solve the equation.

i) $b \times 3 = 15$

$b \times 3 \div 3 = 15 \div 3$

$b = 5$

ii) $b \times 5 = 20$

iii) $b \times 2 = 16$

b) Use the picture to explain why you can divide both sides by 3 to solve the equation $b \times 3 = 6$.

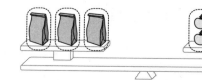

19. Solving Equations—Guess and Check

Finding the value of a variable that makes an equation true is called solving for the variable. Sindi uses a table to solve $2x + 1 = 7$.

x	$2x + 1$	Is equation true?
1	3	✗
2	5	✗
3	7	✓

So $x = 3$ makes the equation true.

1. Complete the table, then solve for x.

a) $3x + 2 = 14$

x	$3x + 2$	True?
1	$3(1) + 2 = 5$	✗
2	$3(2) + 2 = 8$	✗

So $x =$ _____

b) $4x + 3 = 23$

x	$4x + 3$	True?
1	$4(1) + 3 = 7$	✗

So $x =$ _____

c) $5x - 2 = 13$

x	$5x - 2$	True?

So $x =$ _____

2. Replace n with 5 and say whether 5 is too high or too low. Then try a lower or higher number.

a) $3n + 2 = 20$

n	$3n + 2$	Answer
5	$3(5) + 2$	17

5 is _too low_

b) $5n + 1 = 21$

n	$5n + 1$	Answer
5	$5(5) + 1$	

5 is _____

c) $2n + 3 = 15$

n	$2n + 3$	Answer
5		

5 is _____

d) $4n + 3 = 27$

n	$4n + 3$	Answer
5		

5 is _____

e) $5n - 6 = 14$

n	$5n - 6$	Answer
5	$5(5) - 6$	

5 is _____

f) $3n - 3 = 15$

n	$3n - 3$	Answer
5		

5 is _____

3. Solve for n by guessing small values for n, checking, and revising.

a) $3n + 2 = 14$

b) $5n - 2 = 13$

c) $4n - 1 = 15$

d) $6n - 5 = 31$

e) $7n - 2 = 19$

f) $2n + 3 = 9$

20. Equations Involving Fractions

There are 6 apples. Some are in a bag and the other 4 are on a table.

David uses the equation $x + 4 = 6$ to find out how many apples are in the bag.
To solve $x + 4 = 6$, subtract 4 from both sides of the equation.

$$\begin{array}{rcr} x + 4 &=& 6 \\ -4 &=& -4 \\ \hline x &=& 2 \end{array}$$ ← 2 apples are in the bag

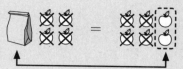

1. Write an equation and then find the number of apples in the bag by solving the equation.

a) $\quad$ = $\quad$

$$\begin{array}{rcr} x + 1 &=& 4 \\ -1 &=& -1 \\ \hline x &=& 3 \end{array}$$

b) $\quad$ = $\quad$

c) $\quad$ = $\quad$

d) $\quad$ = $\quad$

Diba's mother cut a pizza into 6 pieces. She put away some pieces in the fridge and left 4 pieces on the kitchen table.

Diba uses the equation $x + \dfrac{4}{6} = \dfrac{6}{6}$ to find out what fraction of the whole pizza is in the fridge.

$$\begin{array}{rcl} x + \dfrac{4}{6} &=& \dfrac{6}{6} \\[2mm] -\dfrac{4}{6} &=& -\dfrac{4}{6} \\[2mm] \hline x &=& \dfrac{2}{6} \end{array}$$ ← $\dfrac{2}{6}$ of the whole pizza is in the fridge

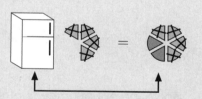

2. Subtract $\dfrac{1}{6}$ from both sides of the equation.

a) $x + \dfrac{1}{6} = \dfrac{6}{6}$

$$\begin{array}{cc} -\dfrac{1}{6} & -\dfrac{1}{6} \\ \hline x = & \boxed{\dfrac{5}{6}} \end{array}$$

b) $x + \dfrac{1}{6} = \dfrac{3}{6}$

$$\begin{array}{cc} -\dfrac{1}{6} & -\dfrac{1}{6} \\ \hline x = & \boxed{} \end{array}$$

c) $\dfrac{4}{6} = x + \dfrac{1}{6}$

$$\begin{array}{cc} -\dfrac{1}{6} & -\dfrac{1}{6} \\ \hline \boxed{} = & x \end{array}$$

d) $\dfrac{5}{6} = x + \dfrac{1}{6}$

$$\begin{array}{cc} -\dfrac{1}{6} & -\dfrac{1}{6} \\ \hline \boxed{} = & x \end{array}$$

3. Solve the equation by subtracting the same number from both sides.

a) $x + \dfrac{1}{5} = \dfrac{3}{5}$

$$\begin{array}{cc} -\dfrac{1}{5} & -\dfrac{1}{5} \\ \hline x = & \dfrac{2}{5} \end{array}$$

b) $x + \dfrac{3}{7} = \dfrac{5}{7}$

c) $\dfrac{8}{10} = x + \dfrac{7}{10}$

BONUS ▶ $\dfrac{2}{3} = x + \dfrac{2}{3}$

4. Replace n with $\frac{1}{4}$ in the expression, then evaluate. Reduce your answer to the lowest terms.

a) $n + \frac{1}{4}$

$= \frac{1}{4} + \frac{1}{4}$

$= \frac{2}{4}$

$= \frac{1}{2}$

b) $n + \frac{3}{4}$

c) $\frac{3}{4} - n$

d) $n - \frac{1}{4}$

5. Replace the variable with the given number, then evaluate.

a) $h + 2\frac{1}{5}$, $h = \frac{2}{5}$

$= \frac{2}{5} + 2\frac{1}{5}$

$= 2\frac{3}{5}$

b) $n + 1\frac{2}{10}$, $n = \frac{3}{10}$

c) $t - \frac{2}{7}$, $t = 3\frac{4}{7}$

d) $m + 2\frac{1}{5}$, $m = \frac{3}{5}$

e) $1\frac{5}{6} - z$, $z = \frac{1}{6}$

f) $n + 5\frac{1}{4}$, $n = 1\frac{3}{4}$

g) $n - 1\frac{1}{10}$, $n = 3\frac{2}{5}$

h) $3\frac{1}{4} - n$, $n = 1\frac{1}{2}$

6. Solve the equation by subtracting or adding the same number to both sides.

a) $x + 1\frac{1}{5} = 4\frac{3}{5}$

$\phantom{x + 1\frac{1}{5}}\; -1\frac{1}{5} \quad -1\frac{1}{5}$

$\overline{}$

$x = 3\frac{2}{5}$

b) $x + 2\frac{3}{7} = 3\frac{5}{7}$

c) $\frac{3}{4} = x + \frac{1}{2}$

d) $2\frac{1}{5} + x = 4\frac{2}{5}$

e) $x - 3\frac{1}{2} = 1\frac{1}{2}$

f) $x - 2\frac{3}{5} = 3\frac{1}{10}$

g) $\frac{8}{6} = x - \frac{2}{3}$

BONUS ▶ $3\frac{2}{5} + x = 4\frac{3}{10}$

21. Decimal Fractions

In a **decimal fraction**, the denominator is a power of ten.

10, 100, 1,000, 10,000, … are **powers of 10**.

Example: $\dfrac{8}{100}$ is a decimal fraction.

5, 26, 111, 700, … are **not powers of 10**.

Example: $\dfrac{8}{700}$ is not a decimal fraction.

1. Circle the decimal fractions.

$\dfrac{3}{10}$ $\qquad$ $\dfrac{25}{100}$ $\qquad$ $\dfrac{333}{1,000}$ $\qquad$ $\dfrac{7}{29}$ $\qquad$ $\dfrac{1}{100}$ $\qquad$ $\dfrac{100}{13}$ $\qquad$ $\dfrac{4}{1,000}$ $\qquad$ $\dfrac{48}{10}$ $\qquad$ $\dfrac{16}{101}$ $\qquad$ $\dfrac{1}{70}$

There are 100 squares on a **hundredths grid**.

1 column $= \dfrac{10}{100} = \dfrac{1}{10} = 1$ tenth

1 square $= \dfrac{1}{100} = 1$ hundredth

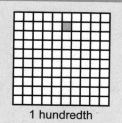

1 one $\qquad$ 1 tenth $\qquad$ 1 hundredth

2. Write two equivalent fractions for the shaded part of the grid.

a)

$\dfrac{2}{10} = \dfrac{}{100}$

b)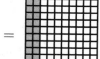

$\dfrac{}{10} = \dfrac{}{100}$

c)

$\dfrac{}{10} = \dfrac{}{100}$

3. Write an equivalent fraction with denominator 100.

a) $\dfrac{8 \times 10}{10 \times 10} = \dfrac{}{100}$

b) $\dfrac{7 \times 10}{10 \times 10} = \dfrac{}{100}$

c) $\dfrac{4}{10} = \dfrac{}{100}$

d) $\dfrac{5}{10} = \dfrac{}{}$

e) $\dfrac{9}{10} = \dfrac{}{}$

f) $\dfrac{2}{10} = \dfrac{}{}$

4. Write an equivalent fraction with denominator 1,000.

a) $\dfrac{8 \times 10}{100 \times 10} = \dfrac{}{1,000}$

b) $\dfrac{7}{100} = \dfrac{}{1,000}$

c) $\dfrac{2}{100} = \dfrac{}{1,000}$

d) $\dfrac{9 \times 100}{10 \times 100} = \dfrac{}{1,000}$

e) $\dfrac{7}{10} = \dfrac{}{1,000}$

f) $\dfrac{4}{10} = \dfrac{}{1,000}$

g) $\dfrac{6}{10} = \dfrac{}{}$

h) $\dfrac{5}{100} = \dfrac{}{}$

i) $\dfrac{1}{100} = \dfrac{}{}$

5. Write the equivalent hundredths and thousandths.

Tenths	$\frac{7}{10}$	$\frac{3}{10}$	$\frac{8}{10}$	$\frac{2}{10}$	$\frac{9}{10}$	$\frac{10}{10}$
Hundredths						
Thousandths						

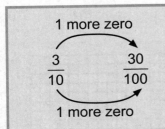 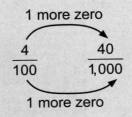 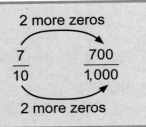

6. How many zeros were added to the denominator? Add the same number of zeros to the numerator.

a) $\dfrac{8}{10} = \dfrac{}{100}$

b) $\dfrac{90}{100} = \dfrac{}{1,000}$

c) $\dfrac{7}{100} = \dfrac{}{1,000}$

d) $\dfrac{4}{10} = \dfrac{}{1,000}$

e) $\dfrac{6}{10} = \dfrac{}{1,000}$

f) $\dfrac{3}{10} = \dfrac{}{100}$

BONUS▶ $\dfrac{40}{1,000} = \dfrac{}{10,000,000}$

7. Write the decimal fraction shown by the shaded part of the grid in four ways.

		$\dfrac{}{100}$	$\dfrac{}{10} + \dfrac{}{100}$	_____ hundredths	_____ tenths _____ hundredths
a)		$\dfrac{23}{100}$	$\dfrac{2}{10} + \dfrac{3}{100}$	__23__ hundredths	__2__ tenths __3__ hundredths
b)				_____ hundredths	_____ tenths _____ hundredths
c)				_____ hundredths	_____ tenths _____ hundredths

To add $\dfrac{9}{10} + \dfrac{4}{100} + \dfrac{8}{1,000}$, change all fractions to thousandths.

$$\dfrac{9 \times 100}{10 \times 100} + \dfrac{4 \times 10}{100 \times 10} + \dfrac{8}{1,000} = \dfrac{900}{1,000} + \dfrac{40}{1,000} + \dfrac{8}{1,000} = \dfrac{948}{1,000}$$

8. Add. Show your work.

a) $\dfrac{5 \times 100}{10 \times 100} + \dfrac{3 \times 10}{100 \times 10} + \dfrac{7}{1,000}$

b) $\dfrac{3 \times 100}{10 \times 100} + \dfrac{8 \times 10}{100 \times 10} + \dfrac{6}{1,000}$

$= \dfrac{500}{1,000} + \dfrac{30}{1,000} + \dfrac{7}{1,000} = \dfrac{537}{1,000}$

$= \dfrac{}{1,000} + \dfrac{}{1,000} + \dfrac{}{1,000} = \dfrac{}{1,000}$

c) $\dfrac{2 \times}{10 \times} + \dfrac{9 \times}{100 \times} + \dfrac{4}{1,000}$

d) $\dfrac{6}{10} + \dfrac{1}{100} + \dfrac{5}{1,000}$

$= \dfrac{}{1,000} + \dfrac{}{1,000} + \dfrac{}{1,000} = \dfrac{}{1,000}$

$= \dfrac{}{1,000} + \dfrac{}{1,000} + \dfrac{}{1,000} = \dfrac{}{1,000}$

9. Write the sum as a sum of fractions with the same denominator.

a) $\dfrac{1}{10} + \dfrac{6}{100} + \dfrac{2}{1,000} = \dfrac{100}{1,000} + \dfrac{60}{1,000} + \dfrac{2}{1,000} = \dfrac{162}{1,000}$

b) $\dfrac{2}{10} + \dfrac{7}{100} + \dfrac{5}{1,000} =$

c) $\dfrac{6}{10} + \dfrac{3}{100} + \dfrac{4}{1,000} =$

10. Add the tenths and hundredths in your head.

a) $\dfrac{1}{10} + \dfrac{9}{100} = \underline{\qquad}$

b) $\dfrac{6}{10} + \dfrac{7}{100} = \underline{\qquad}$

c) $\dfrac{7}{10} + \dfrac{2}{100} = \underline{\qquad}$

d) $\dfrac{1}{10} + \dfrac{3}{100} = \underline{\qquad}$

11. Add in your head.

a) $\dfrac{9}{10} + \dfrac{6}{100} + \dfrac{7}{1,000} =$

b) $\dfrac{4}{10} + \dfrac{4}{100} + \dfrac{4}{1,000} =$

c) $\dfrac{5}{10} + \dfrac{6}{1,000} =$

d) $\dfrac{1}{100} + \dfrac{9}{1,000} =$

e) $\dfrac{9}{100} + \dfrac{1}{1,000} =$

f) $\dfrac{8}{10} + \dfrac{8}{1,000} =$

22. Place Value and Decimals

Decimals are a way to record place values based on decimal fractions.

3 hundreds + 6 tens + 5 ones

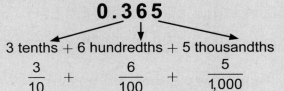

3 tenths + 6 hundredths + 5 thousandths

$$\frac{3}{10} \quad + \quad \frac{6}{100} \quad + \quad \frac{5}{1,000}$$

1. Write the decimal as a sum of a whole number and decimal fractions.

a) $2.17 = \underline{\ 2\ } + \frac{1}{10} + \frac{7}{100}$

b) $3.24 = \underline{\quad} + \frac{}{10} + \frac{}{100}$

c) $5.79 = \underline{\quad} + \frac{}{10} + \frac{}{100}$

d) $6.87 = \underline{\quad} + \frac{}{10} + \frac{}{100}$

e) $0.38 = \underline{\quad} + \frac{}{10} + \frac{}{100}$

f) $9.51 = \underline{\quad} + \frac{}{10} + \frac{}{100}$

g) $3.206 = \underline{\quad} + \frac{}{10} + \frac{}{100} + \frac{}{1,000}$

h) $1.532 = \underline{\quad} + \frac{}{10} + \frac{}{100} + \frac{}{1,000}$

i) $6.521 = \underline{\quad} + \frac{}{10} + \frac{}{100} + \frac{}{1,000}$

j) $7.025 = \underline{\quad} + \frac{}{10} + \frac{}{100} + \frac{}{1,000}$

2. Write the decimal as a sum of a whole number and decimal fractions.
   Do not write the fractions with a numerator of 0.

a) $4.017 = \underline{\ 4\ } + \frac{1}{100} + \frac{7}{1,000}$

b) $7.204 = \underline{\quad} + \frac{}{10} + \frac{}{1,000}$

c) $0.709 =$

d) $6.087 =$

e) $0.008 =$

f) $4.001 =$

3. What is the value of the 9 in each decimal? Write the answer two ways.

a) $0.497 \ \frac{9}{100}$ or $\underline{9\ hundredths}$

b) $8.439 \ \underline{\frac{9}{\ \ }}$ or $9 \underline{\qquad}$

c) $1.923 \ \underline{\frac{9}{\ \ }}$ or $\underline{\qquad}$

d) $0.907 \ \underline{\frac{9}{\ \ }}$ or $\underline{\qquad}$

e) $0.479 \ \underline{\quad}$ or $\underline{\qquad}$

f) $5.491 \ \underline{\quad}$ or $\underline{\qquad}$

g) $3.904 \ \underline{\quad}$ or $\underline{\qquad}$

h) $7.609 \ \underline{\quad}$ or $\underline{\qquad}$

4. Write the decimal fractions in the place value chart, then write the number as a decimal.

a) $\dfrac{3}{10} = 0.\underline{\ 3\ }$

Ones	Tenths
0	3

b) $\dfrac{6}{10} = 0.\underline{\ \ \ \ }$

Ones	Tenths

c) $\dfrac{6}{10} + \dfrac{5}{100} = \underline{\ 0\ }.\underline{\ \ \ }\ \underline{\ \ \ }$

Ones	Tenths	Hundredths
0		

d) $\dfrac{5}{10} + \dfrac{4}{100} = \underline{\ \ \ }.\underline{\ \ \ }\ \underline{\ \ \ }$

Ones	Tenths	Hundredths

e) $\dfrac{1}{10} + \dfrac{8}{100} = \underline{\ \ \ }.\underline{\ \ \ }\ \underline{\ \ \ }$

Ones	Tenths	Hundredths
0		

f) $\dfrac{2}{10} + \dfrac{4}{100} + \dfrac{3}{1,000} = \underline{\ \ \ }.\underline{\ \ \ }\ \underline{\ \ \ }\ \underline{\ \ \ }$

Ones	Tenths	Hundredths	Thousandths
0	2	4	3

g) $\dfrac{1}{10} + \dfrac{5}{100} + \dfrac{4}{1,000} = \underline{\ \ \ }.\underline{\ \ \ }\ \underline{\ \ \ }\ \underline{\ \ \ }$

Ones	Tenths	Hundredths	Thousandths
0			

h) $3 + \dfrac{1}{10} + \dfrac{8}{100} = \underline{\ 3\ }.\underline{\ \ \ }\ \underline{\ \ \ }$

Ones	Tenths	Hundredths
3		

i) $7 + \dfrac{3}{100} + \dfrac{5}{1,000} = \underline{\ \ \ }.\underline{\ \ \ }\ \underline{\ \ \ }\ \underline{\ \ \ }$

Ones	Tenths	Hundredths	Thousandths

j) $30 + 4 + \dfrac{2}{100} = \underline{\ \ \ }\ \underline{\ \ \ }.\underline{\ \ \ }\ \underline{\ \ \ }$

Tens	Ones	Tenths	Hundredths

5. The decimal point is between the _____ and _____ place values.

6. Write the decimal in the place value chart.

	Ones	Tenths	Hundredths	Thousandths
a) 0.512	0	5	1	2
b) 0.905				
c) 0.3				
d) 1.536				
e) 4.763				
f) 0.8				
g) 3.48				

7. Underline the smallest place value. Write the decimal in words.

a) 0.6 = _six tenths_____

b) 0.07 = _____

c) 0.005 = _____

d) 0.02 = _____

e) 0.3 = _____

f) 0.004 = _____

8. Write the decimal in expanded form.

a) 0.407 = _0_ ones + _4_ tenths + _0_ hundredths + _7_ thousandths

b) 5.163 = _5_ ones + ____ tenth + ____ hundredths + ____ thousandths

c) 3.08 = ____ ones + ____ tenths + ____ hundredths

d) 0.76 = ____ ones + ____ tenths + ____ hundredths

e) 8.201 = ____ ones + ____ tenths + ____ hundredths + ____ thousandth

9. Write the number in expanded form as a decimal.

a) 0 ones + 3 tenths + 5 hundredths + 2 thousandths = _0_ . ____ ____ ____

b) 7 ones + 4 tenths + 1 hundredth + 6 thousandths = _7_ . ____ ____ ____

c) 4 ones + 5 tenths = ____ . ____

d) 9 ones + 8 tenths + 2 hundredths = ____ . ____ ____

e) 5 tenths + 3 thousandths = _0_ . ____ ____ ____

f) 3 hundredths + 5 thousandths = ____ . ____ ____ ____

A **dime** is **one tenth** of a dollar. A **penny** is **one hundredth** of a dollar.

---

10. a) Express the value of each decimal in four ways.
Hint: Put a zero in the hundredths place if there are no hundredths.

i) 0.63 _____ dimes _____ pennies

_____ tenths _____ hundredths

_____ pennies

_____ hundredths

ii) 0.8 _____ dimes _____ pennies

_____ tenths _____ hundredths

_____ pennies

_____ hundredths

b) George says that 0.63 is greater than 0.8 because 63 is greater than 8.
Can you explain his mistake?

11. Put a decimal point in each number so that the digit 7 has the value $\frac{7}{10}$.

a) 5 7 2

b) 1 0 7

c) 2 8 7 5 9

d) 1 7

---

23. Positive and Negative Decimals

The whole-number part of a decimal
is the part **to the left** of the decimal point.

decimal point

$$7.348$$

whole-number part   fractional part

1. Underline the whole-number part of the decimal.

   a) <u>36</u>.497   b) 196.4   c) 25.76   d) 8.036   e) 0.38

2. Write the number as a decimal.

   a) 2 tens + 4 ones + 3 tenths + 5 hundredths + 2 thousandths = ___ ___ . ___ ___ ___

   b) 9 ones + 4 tenths + 1 hundredth + 6 thousandths = _____

   c) 4 tens + 8 ones + 7 tenths + 2 hundredths = _____

3. Write the decimal in the place value chart.

	Hundreds	Tens	Ones	Tenths	Hundredths	Thousandths
a) 17.34		1	7	3	4	
b) 8.675						
c) 250.93						
d) 49.007						

4. Write the whole number and how many hundredths or thousandths.

   a) 6.45   ____six____ and _____forty-five_____ hundredths

   b) 1.32   _____ and _____ hundredths

   c) 86.007   _____ and _____ thousandths

   d) 7.052   _____ and _____ thousandths

   e) 20.104   _____ and _____ thousandths

5. Write the decimal in words.

   a) 6.8 ___six and eight tenths_____

   b) 3.02 _____

   c) 25.79 _____

   d) 15.285 _____

A decimal can be written as a mixed number. Example: $3.75 = 3\frac{75}{100}$

6. Write the number represented on the grids in three ways.

a)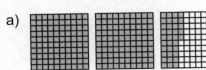

_2_ ones _35_ hundredths   _2_ . _3_ _5_   _2_ $\frac{35}{100}$

b)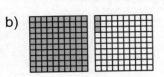

____ one ____ hundredths   ____ . ____ ____   ____ $\overline{}$ $\frac{}{100}$

c)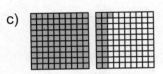

____ one ____ hundredths   ____ . ____ ____   ____ $\overline{}$ $\frac{}{100}$

7. Write a mixed number for the decimal.

a) $2.8 =$ b) $3.04 =$ c) $7.068 =$

When two numbers are equal, so are their opposites!

Example: $7.4 = 7\frac{4}{10}$ so $-7.4 = -7\frac{4}{10}$

8. Write a negative mixed number for the negative decimal.

a) -3.21 b) -1.62 c) -8.6 d) -9.137 e) -31.76 f) -82.505

$-3\frac{21}{100}$

9. Write a decimal for the mixed number.

a) $+2\frac{17}{100}$ b) $-1\frac{67}{100}$ c) $+76\frac{7}{10}$ d) $-5\frac{375}{1,000}$ e) $-3\frac{9}{10}$ f) $29\frac{5}{1,000}$

When the whole-number part of the decimal is zero, you don't have to write the 0.

Example: 0.25 can be written as .25.

10. Circle the numbers that are equal to four tenths.

$\frac{4}{1,000}$ $\frac{4}{10}$ $\frac{4}{100}$ four hundredths   four tens

.04   0.4   0.04   .4   40   400

11. Write five tenths in at least three ways.

12. Change the improper fraction into a mixed number by shading the correct number of pieces.

a)

$\dfrac{27}{10}$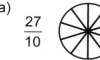

Mixed number: _____

b)

$\dfrac{31}{10}$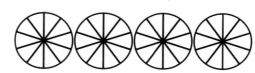

Mixed number: _____

13. Fill in the blanks. Then write the mixed number.

a) $48 \div 10 =$ _____ R _____ so $\dfrac{48}{10} = 4\dfrac{8}{10}$

b) $67 \div 10 =$ _____ R _____ so $\dfrac{67}{10} =$

c) $99 \div 10 =$ _____ R _____ so $\dfrac{99}{10} =$

d) $745 \div 100 =$ _____ R _____ so $\dfrac{745}{100} =$

14. Write the improper fraction as a mixed number and then as a decimal.

a) $\dfrac{23}{10} = \boxed{2\dfrac{3}{10}} = \underline{\ 2.3\ }$

b) $\dfrac{59}{10} = \boxed{} =$ _____

c) $\dfrac{121}{100} = \boxed{} =$ _____

d) $\dfrac{7{,}452}{100} = \boxed{} =$ _____

To write the improper fraction $\dfrac{43{,}725}{100}$ as a decimal:
Write the numerator without the commas.
Then place the decimal point to match the
denominator of the fraction.

$$\dfrac{43{,}725}{\underline{100}} = 437.\underline{25}$$

2 zeros   2 digits

---

15. Write the improper fraction as a decimal.

a) $\dfrac{74}{10} = \underline{\ 7.4\ }$

b) $\dfrac{684}{100} =$ _____

c) $\dfrac{835}{100} =$ _____

d) $\dfrac{5{,}374}{10} =$ _____

e) $\dfrac{1{,}902}{100} =$ _____

BONUS ▶ $\dfrac{285{,}376}{10{,}000} =$ _____

16. Write the negative improper fraction as a negative decimal.

a) $-\dfrac{89}{10} = \underline{\ -8.9\ }$

b) $-\dfrac{729}{10} =$ _____

c) $-\dfrac{642}{100} =$ _____

d) $-\dfrac{307}{10} =$ _____

e) $-\dfrac{3{,}704}{100} =$ _____

BONUS ▶ $-\dfrac{432{,}095}{10{,}000} =$ _____

---

24. Equivalent Fractions and Decimals

1. Complete the chart.

	Drawing	Fraction	Decimal	Equivalent Decimal	Equivalent Decimal Fraction	Drawing
a)		$\frac{5}{10}$	0.5	0.50	$\frac{50}{100}$	
b)		$\frac{}{10}$	__.__	__.__ __	$\frac{}{100}$	
c)						

2. Write equivalent decimal fractions for the decimal.

a) $0.3 = \frac{3}{10} = \frac{30}{100} = \frac{300}{1,000}$

b) $.9 = \frac{}{10} = \frac{}{100} = \frac{}{1,000}$

c) $0.04 = \frac{}{100} = \frac{}{1,000}$

d) $0.09 = \frac{}{100} = \frac{}{1,000}$

3. Fill in the missing numbers. Remember: $\frac{1}{10} = \frac{10}{100} = \frac{100}{1,000}$

a) $0.8 = \frac{8}{10} = \frac{}{100} = 0.80$

b) $0.5 = \frac{5}{10} = \frac{}{100} = \frac{}{1,000} = 0.500$

c) $0.\underline{\ \ } = \frac{}{10} = \frac{40}{100} = 0.\underline{\ \ }\ \underline{\ \ }$

d) $0.\underline{\ \ } = \frac{}{10} = \frac{}{100} = \frac{700}{1,000} = 0.\underline{\ \ }\ \underline{\ \ }\ \underline{\ \ }$

e) $0.03 = \frac{3}{100} = \frac{}{1,000} = 0.030$

f) $0.\underline{\ \ }\ \underline{\ \ } = \frac{2}{100} = \frac{}{1,000} = 0.020$

4. Write each decimal as a sum of decimal fractions.

a) $0.27 = \frac{2}{10} + \frac{7}{100} = \frac{27}{100}$

b) $0.40 = \frac{}{10} + \frac{}{100} = \frac{}{100}$

c) $.06 = \frac{}{10} + \frac{}{100} = \frac{}{100}$

d) $0.532 = \frac{}{10} + \frac{}{100} + \frac{}{1,000} = \frac{}{1,000}$

e) $0.918 = \dfrac{}{10} + \dfrac{}{100} + \dfrac{}{1,000} = \dfrac{}{1,000}$

f) $.702 = \dfrac{}{10} + \dfrac{}{100} + \dfrac{}{1,000} = \dfrac{}{1,000}$

g) $0.036 = \dfrac{}{10} + \dfrac{}{100} + \dfrac{}{1,000} = \dfrac{}{1,000}$

h) $0.003 = \dfrac{}{10} + \dfrac{}{100} + \dfrac{}{1,000} = \dfrac{}{1,000}$

5. Write the decimal in expanded form and as a fraction with denominator 1,000.

	Decimal	Expanded Form	Fraction with Denominator 1,000
a)	0.382	$\dfrac{3}{10} + \dfrac{8}{100} + \dfrac{2}{1,000}$	$\dfrac{382}{1,000}$
b)	0.204		
c)	0.086		
d)	0.73		$\dfrac{}{1,000}$

6. Write the decimal in expanded form using words and write the total number of thousandths.

	Decimal	Expanded Form	Thousandths
a)	0.328	___3___ tenths ___2___ hundredths ___8___ thousandths	___328___ thousandths
b)	0.409	_____ tenths _____ hundredths _____ thousandths	_____ thousandths
c)	0.098	_____ tenths _____ hundredths _____ thousandths	_____ thousandths
d)	0.35	_____ tenths _____ hundredths _____ thousandths	_____ thousandths

> If a decimal is equivalent to a fraction, their opposites are equivalent too.
>
> Example: $0.275 = \dfrac{275}{1,000}$, so $-0.275 = -\dfrac{275}{1,000}$

7. Write the equivalent fractions.

a) $0.34 = \dfrac{34}{100}$, so $-0.34 = -\dfrac{}{100}$

b) $0.7 = \dfrac{}{10}$, so $-0.7 = -\dfrac{}{10}$

c) $0.06 = \dfrac{}{100}$, so $-0.06 = -\dfrac{}{100}$

d) $0.804 = \dfrac{}{1,000}$, so $-0.804 = -\dfrac{}{1,000}$

e) $-0.5 =$

f) $-0.74 =$

g) $-0.605 =$

h) $-0.004 =$

25. Ordering Decimals

1. Write an equivalent fraction.

   a) $\dfrac{4}{10} = \dfrac{}{100}$

   b) $\dfrac{52}{100} = \dfrac{}{1,000}$

   c) $\dfrac{70}{100} = \dfrac{}{1,000}$

   d) $\dfrac{7}{100} = \dfrac{}{1,000}$

   e) $\dfrac{3}{100} = \dfrac{}{1,000}$

   f) $\dfrac{6}{10} = \dfrac{}{1,000}$

   g) $\dfrac{9}{10} = \dfrac{}{1,000}$

   h) $\dfrac{1}{100} = \dfrac{}{1,000}$

2. Fill in the blank.

   a) 3 tenths = _____ hundredths

   b) 36 hundredths = _____ thousandths

   c) 9 tenths = _____ thousandths

   d) 5 hundredths = _____ thousandths

   e) 60 hundredths = _____ thousandths

   f) 7 tenths = _____ hundredths

3. Change both decimals to fractions with the same denominator.
   Then write < (less than) or > (greater than) to show which decimal is greater.

   a)

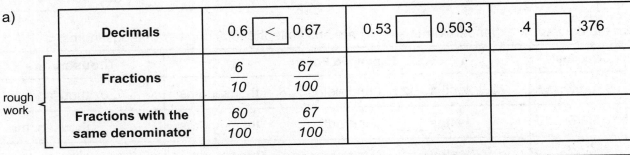

	Decimals	0.6 $\boxed{<}$ 0.67	0.53 $\square$ 0.503	.4 $\square$ .376
rough work	Fractions	$\dfrac{6}{10}$ $\dfrac{67}{100}$		
	Fractions with the same denominator	$\dfrac{60}{100}$ $\dfrac{67}{100}$		

   b)

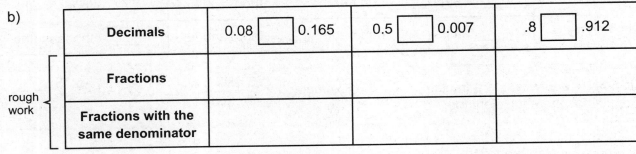

	Decimals	0.08 $\square$ 0.165	0.5 $\square$ 0.007	.8 $\square$ .912
rough work	Fractions			
	Fractions with the same denominator			

> To compare decimals, Rena adds zeros so all numbers have the same number of digits after the decimal point.
>
> Example: .6 and .42   Add a zero to .6:   .6 ⟶ .60
> 60 hundredths are greater than 42 hundredths, so .6 is greater than .42.

4. Add zeros to compare the decimals. Circle the greatest decimal.

   a) .76   (.80)

   b) 0.7   .08

   c) .6   .503

   d) .49   .623   .5

   e) .4   .32   .41

   f) 0.720   0.80   .716

   g) 3.53   .4573   .66

   h) 12.31   .230   .12

   i) 2.5   .25   2.05

5. Write the numbers in the place value chart. Order the numbers from greatest to least.

a) 37.03, 3.706, 7.306, 6.73

Tens	Ones	Tenths	Hundredths	Thousandths
3	7	0	3	

_____ , _____ , _____ , _____

b) 0.654, 0.555, 0.655, 0.554

Ones	Tenths	Hundredths	Thousandths

_____ , _____ , _____ , _____

6. Arrange the numbers in increasing order.

a) 3.67, 3.076, 367

_____ , _____ , _____

b) 0.004, 0.040, 0.041

_____ , _____ , _____

7. a) Write a decimal between 0.457 and 0.5.

b) Write five decimals between −1.33 and −1.32.

8. Write the numbers in the place value chart. Order the numbers from least to greatest.

a) −6.43, −6.331, −6.33, −6.4

+/−	Ones	Tenths	Hundredths	Thousandths

_____ , _____ , _____ , _____

b) −0.9, −0.09, −0.099, −1.9

+/−	Ones	Tenths	Hundredths	Thousandths

_____ , _____ , _____ , _____

c) −1.999, 2.01, −1.9, 2.0

+/−	Ones	Tenths	Hundredths	Thousandths

_____ , _____ , _____ , _____

d) 14.05, −15.04, −1.04, 5.4

+/−	Tens	Ones	Tenths	Hundredths

_____ , _____ , _____ , _____

26. Comparing Decimal Fractions and Decimals

The number line is divided into tenths. Point A is at $\frac{8}{10} = 0.8$. Point B is at $-\frac{8}{10} = -0.8$.

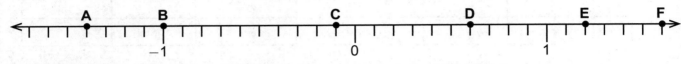

1. Write a decimal and a fraction for each point on the number line.

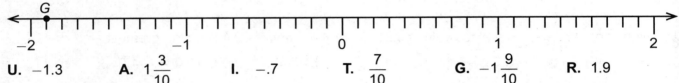

	A	B	C	D	E	F
Decimal	−1.4					
Fraction	$-1\frac{4}{10}$					

2. Mark each point with a dot and the correct letter. The letters spell the word _____.

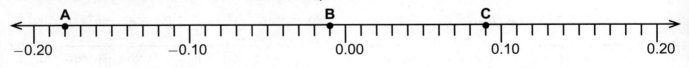

U. −1.3   **A.** $1\frac{3}{10}$ **I.** −.7   **T.** $\frac{7}{10}$ **G.** $-1\frac{9}{10}$ **R.** 1.9

The number line is divided into hundredths. Point A is at $\frac{26}{100} = 0.26$.

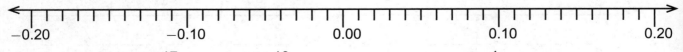

3. Write a decimal fraction and a decimal for each point on the number line

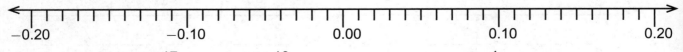

A. _____ _____   **B.** _____ _____   **C.** _____ _____

4. Mark each point on the number line with a dot and the correct letter.

What word do the letters spell? _____.

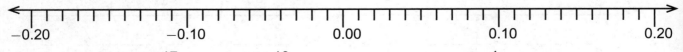

R. .17   **W.** $-\frac{17}{100}$ **I.** $-\frac{10}{100}$ **E.** 0.10   **T.** $\frac{1}{100}$ **N.** −.01

5. Cross out the labels for the points that are incorrect. Write the correct number.

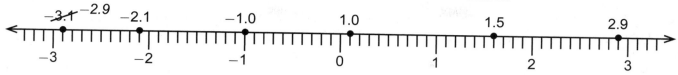

6. Arrange the numbers from least to greatest.

a) $1\dfrac{15}{1,000}$, $-\dfrac{15}{1,000}$, $\dfrac{995}{1,000}$

_____ , _____ , _____

b) $-\dfrac{207}{1,000}$, $\dfrac{27}{100}$, $-\dfrac{3}{10}$

_____ , _____ , _____

7. Change all of the decimals to fractions with denominator 100. Then write the numbers in order from greatest to least.

a) .3   −.3 $-\dfrac{3}{100}$ $\dfrac{30}{100}$

____ ____ ____ ____

____ > ____ > ____ ____

b) $-\dfrac{37}{100}$ .8   −.4

____ ____ ____

____ > ____ > ____

c) −1.4 $1\dfrac{4}{100}$ $\dfrac{14}{100}$

____ ____ ____

____ > ____ > ____

8. Use the numbers 100 and 1,000 as denominators to make the statement true.

a) $\dfrac{7}{100} > \dfrac{7}{1,000}$

b) $\dfrac{7}{\underline{\quad}} < \dfrac{7}{\underline{\quad}}$

c) $-\dfrac{7}{\underline{\quad}} > -\dfrac{7}{\underline{\quad}}$

d) $-\dfrac{7}{\underline{\quad}} < -\dfrac{7}{\underline{\quad}}$

9. Use the numbers 3 and 40 as numerators to make the statement true.

a) $\dfrac{3}{10} < \dfrac{40}{100}$

b) $\dfrac{\underline{\quad}}{1,000} > \dfrac{\underline{\quad}}{100}$

c) $-\dfrac{\underline{\quad}}{100} < -\dfrac{\underline{\quad}}{1,000}$

d) $-\dfrac{\underline{\quad}}{10} > -\dfrac{\underline{\quad}}{100}$

10. a) The American toad hibernates underground during the winter. The colder the weather on average, the deeper the toad burrows. The average winter temperature is −0.5°F where Toad A lives, and −1.5°F where Toad B lives. Which toad's burrow is deeper? _____

b) The American bullfrog hibernates in the water near the bottom of ponds. The western pond turtle digs into the mud under ponds. The bottom of a pond is at −2.53 m. Which animal could be found at each depth?

−2.35 m _____ and −3.25 m _____

11. Use all the digits 5, 6, 7, and 1 to write a number between the given numbers.

a) 5.617 < _____ < 5.761

b) −57.16 < _____ < −51.76

27. Multi-Digit Addition

1. Add the numbers below by drawing base ten materials and by adding the digits.
   Use the base ten materials to show how to combine the numbers and how to regroup.

a) 26 + 36

	With Base Ten Materials		With Numerals	
	Tens	Ones	Tens	Ones
26	(2 tens)	(6 ones)	2	6
36	(3 tens)	(6 ones)	3	6
sum	(5 tens)	(12 ones) regroup 10 ones as 1 ten	5	12
	(6 tens)	(2 ones) after regrouping	6	2

b) 57 + 27

	With Base Ten Materials		With Numerals	
	Tens	Ones	Tens	Ones

2. Add the ones digits. Show how you would regroup 10 ones as 1 ten.

   tens go here

a)
```
   [1]
   1 6
 + 1 7
   [3]
```
ones go here

b)
```
   [ ]
   2 4
 + 3 6
   [ ]
```

c)
```
   [ ]
   5 7
 + 1 9
   [ ]
```

d)
```
   [ ]
   7 3
 + 1 9
   [ ]
```

e)
```
   [ ]
   5 7
 + 3 5
   [ ]
```

3. Use regrouping to add the numbers.

a)
```
  1
  4 6
 + 2 5
  7 1
```

b)
```
  3 3
 + 4 8
```

c)
```
  7 2
 + 1 9
```

d)
```
  8 5
 + 1 7
```

e)
```
  4 7
 + 2 6
```

f)
```
  3 8
 + 4 3
```

g)
```
  6 9
 +   9
```

h)
```
  7 4
 + 1 9
```

i)
```
  4 3
 + 3 9
```

j)
```
  6 8
 + 2 9
```

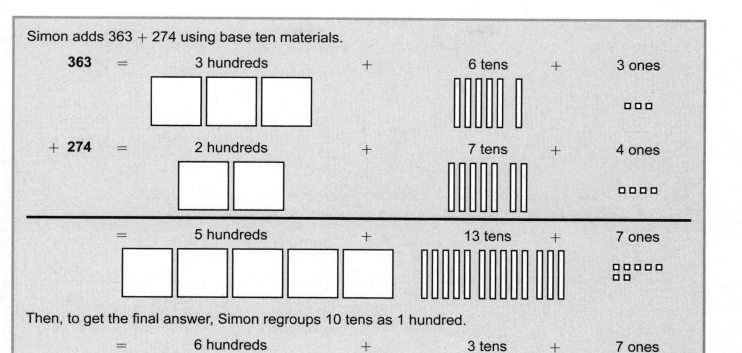

Simon adds 363 + 274 using base ten materials.

363 = 3 hundreds + 6 tens + 3 ones

+ 274 = 2 hundreds + 7 tens + 4 ones

= 5 hundreds + 13 tens + 7 ones

Then, to get the final answer, Simon regroups 10 tens as 1 hundred.

= 6 hundreds + 3 tens + 7 ones

So 363 + 274 = 637.

4. Add the numbers below, either by using base ten materials or by drawing a picture in your notebook. Record your work here.

483   _____ hundreds + _____ tens + _____ ones

+ 245   + _____ hundreds + _____ tens + _____ ones

           = _____ hundreds + _____ tens + _____ ones

after regrouping   = _____ hundreds + _____ tens + _____ ones

5. Add. You will need to regroup.

a)
```
    1
  3 6 4
+ 2 5 3
───────
    1 7
```

b)
```
  □
  5 7 1
+ 2 5 5
───────
```

c)
```
  □
  6 5 2
+   9 4
───────
```

d)
```
  □
  3 6 2
+ 4 8 2
───────
```

6. Add, regrouping where necessary.

a)
```
  1 6 8
+ 3 2 3
───────
```

b)
```
  2 5 5
+ 3 6 2
───────
```

c)
```
  3 9 5
+ 1 2 3
───────
```

d)
```
  4 6 5
+ 1 5 9
───────
```

7. Add by lining the numbers up correctly in the grid.

a) 449 + 346

	4	4	9
+	3	4	6

b) 273 + 456

+			

c) 832 + 109

+			

d) 347 + 72

+			

8. Add the numbers below, either by using base ten materials or by drawing a picture in your notebook. Record your work here. (Use 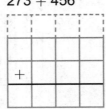 to show a thousand.)

5,486   _____ thousands + _____ hundreds + _____ tens + _____ ones

+ 3,621   + _____ thousands + _____ hundreds + _____ tens + _____ ones

     = _____ thousands + _____ hundreds + _____ tens + _____ ones,

after regrouping   = _____ thousands + _____ hundreds + _____ tens + _____ ones

9. Add. You will need to regroup hundreds as thousands.

a)
```
  [1]
  4 6 8 3
+ 2 7 1 2
---------
  7 3 9 5
```

b)
```
  [ ]
  2 5 3 7
+ 4 6 2 1
---------
```

c)
```
  [ ]
  8 6 5 4
+   7 2 4
---------
```

d)
```
  [ ]
  3 1 7 4
+ 4 9 2 3
---------
```

10. Add. You will need to regroup tens as hundreds.

a)
```
  [ ]
  8 5 6 3
+ 1 3 5 1
---------
```

b)
```
  [ ]
  4 4 8 7
+ 2 3 5 1
---------
```

c)
```
  [ ]
  3 6 8 3
+ 3 1 3 2
---------
```

d)
```
  [ ]
  2 4 7 8
+   2 7 1
---------
```

11. Add, regrouping where necessary.

a)
```
  5 8 4 6
+ 1 1 3 5
---------
```

b)
```
  3 5 6 4
+ 2 8 1 3
---------
```

c)
```
  7 3 2 4 6
+ 1 8 3 8 2
-----------
```

d)
```
  2 3 5 2 7 5
+ 5 1 2 9 1 3
-------------
```

12. a) Camile cycled 2,357 km one year and 5,753 km the next.
How many kilometers did she cycle altogether?

b) Two nearby towns have populations of 442,670 and 564,839.
What is the total population of both towns?

28. Multi-Digit Subtraction

Mark subtracts 54 − 17 using base ten materials.

Step 1:
Mark represents 54 with base ten materials.

Step 2:
7 (the ones digit of 17) is greater than 4 (the ones digit of 54) so Mark regroups a tens block as 10 ones.

Step 3:
Mark subtracts 17 (he takes away 1 tens block and 7 ones).

Tens	Ones
5	4

Tens	Ones
4	14

Tens	Ones
3	7

Here is how Mark uses numerals to show his work:

$$\begin{array}{r} 5\,4 \\ -\,1\,7 \\ \hline \end{array}$$

Here is how Mark shows the regrouping.

$$\begin{array}{r} {}^{4}\!\!\!\not5\ {}^{14}\!\!\!\not4 \\ -\,1\ 7 \\ \hline \end{array}$$

And now Mark can subtract 17.

$$\begin{array}{r} {}^{4}\!\!\!\not5\ {}^{14}\!\!\!\not4 \\ -\,1\ 7 \\ \hline 3\ 7 \end{array}$$

1. In these questions, Mark doesn't have enough ones to subtract. Help him by regrouping a tens block as 10 ones. Show how he would rewrite his subtraction statement.

a) 53 − 36

Tens	Ones
5	3

Tens	Ones
4	13

	5	3
−	3	6

	4	13
	$\not5$	$\not3$
−	3	6

b) 65 − 29

Tens	Ones
6	5

Tens	Ones

	6	5
−	2	9

	6	5
−	2	9

2. Subtract by regrouping.

a)

	7	12
	$\not8$	$\not2$
−	3	7
	4	5

b)

	5	4
−	2	6

c)

	7	5
−	3	8

d)

	4	1
−	2	3

e)

	6	7
−	4	9

3. Subtract by regrouping 1 hundred as 10 tens.

a)

	5	13	
	$\not6$	$\not3$	8
−	4	5	3

b)

	8	5	4
−	3	7	2

c)

	7	5	5
−	3	8	2

d)

	4	2	3
−	1	8	2

4. Subtract by regrouping 1 ten as 10 ones.

a)
	7	14
7	8̸	4̸
− 2	4	8

b)
3	4	3
− 2	1	9

c)
8	2	5
− 5	1	7

d)
6	7	1
− 3	1	6

Sometimes you need to regroup twice.

Example:

Step 1:

2 16
8 8̸ 6̸
− 3 5 8

Step 2:

2 16
8 8̸ 6̸
− 3 5 8
8

Step 3:

12
7 2̸ 16
8̸ 8̸ 6̸
− 3 5 8
8

Step 4:

12
7 2̸ 16
8̸ 8̸ 6̸
− 3 5 8
7 8

Step 5:

12
7 2̸ 16
8̸ 8̸ 6̸
− 3 5 8
4 7 8

5. Subtract, regrouping twice.

a)
9	3	4
− 4	5	6

b)
7	4	7
− 2	6	9

c)
5	3	2
−	5	9

d)
8	9	2	9
− 4	9	5	8

6. a) The Nile River is about 6,690 km long and the Amazon River is 6,440 km long. How much longer is the Nile River than the Amazon River?

b) A box turtle can live 100 years. A rabbit can live 15 years. How much longer than a rabbit can a box turtle live?

Sometimes you need to regroup three times (regroup 1 ten as 10 ones, 1 hundred as 10 tens, and 1 thousand as 10 hundreds).

Example:

Step 1:

1 13
6 4 2̸ 3̸
− 3 7 4 6

Step 2:

1 13
6 4 2̸ 3̸
− 3 7 4 6
7

Step 3:

11
3 1̸ 13
6 4̸ 2̸ 3̸
− 3 7 4 6
7 7

Step 4:

13 11
5 3̸ 1̸ 13
6̸ 4̸ 2̸ 3̸
− 3 7 4 6
6 7 7

Step 5:

13 11
5 3̸ 1̸ 13
6̸ 4̸ 2̸ 3̸
− 3 7 4 6
2 6 7 7

7. Subtract, regrouping three times.

a)
8	7	2	5
− 4	9	5	8

b)
6	4	3	7
− 2	6	7	8

c)
4	5	6	3
− 1	7	9	5

d)
7	8	4	3
− 4	8	6	5

JUMP Math Accumula

8. In the questions below, you will have to regroup *two*, *three*, or *four* times.

Example:

Step 1:

```
   0  10
   X  Ø  0  0
 −    7  5  6
```

Step 2:

```
       9
   0  1̶0  10
   X  Ø  Ø  0
 −    7  5  6
```

Step 3:

```
       9  9
   0  1̶0  1̶0  10
   X  Ø  Ø  Ø
 −    7  5  6
```

Step 4:

```
       9  9
   0  1̶0  1̶0  10
   X  Ø  Ø  Ø
 −    7  5  6
   ─────────────
      2  4  4
```

a)
	1	0	0	0
−		4	6	8

b)
	1	0	0
−		3	2

c)
	1	0	0	0	0
−		6	4	8	6

d)
	1	0	0	0	0
−		5	1	1	1

9. A school has 150 students.
Eighty of the students are boys.
How many are girls?

10. Raj has 150 stamps.
Marina has 12 fewer stamps than Raj.
Cedric has 15 more stamps than Raj.
How many stamps do the children have altogether?

11. A grocery store had 480 cans of soup.
In one week, the store sold

- 212 cans of tomato soup
- 57 cans of chicken soup
- 43 cans of mushroom soup

How many cans were left?

12. a) The Washington Monument is 555 ft tall. The Capitol Building is 289 ft tall. How many feet taller than the Capitol is the Washington Monument?

b) The construction of the Capitol building in Washington, DC, started in 1791. How many years ago was that?

c) The population of Washington, DC, in 1900 was 278,718. In 2000, its population was 572,059. How much did the population of Washington, DC, grow over 100 years?

29. Adding and Subtracting Decimals

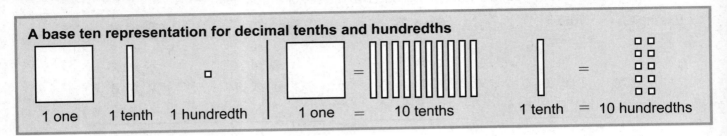

A base ten representation for decimal tenths and hundredths

1 one   1 tenth   1 hundredth | 1 one = 10 tenths   1 tenth = 10 hundredths

1. Regroup every 10 tenths as 1 one.

a)

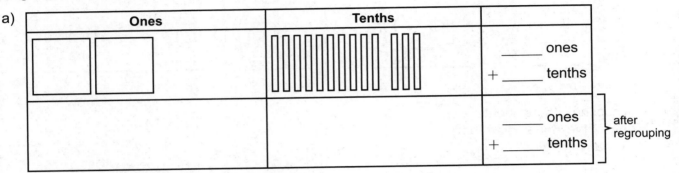

Ones	Tenths	
		_____ ones + _____ tenths
		_____ ones + _____ tenths

after regrouping

b) 27 tenths = _____ ones + _____ tenths   c) 36 tenths = _____ ones + _____ tenths

d) 19 tenths = _____ one + _____ tenths   e) 73 tenths = _____ ones + _____ tenths

2. Regroup so that each place value has a single digit.

a) 2 ones + 14 tenths = ___3___ ones + ___4___ tenths

b) 6 tenths + 17 hundredths = _____ tenths + _____ hundredths

c) 5 hundredths + 11 thousandths = _____ hundredths + _____ thousandth

d) 3 hundredths + 10 thousandths = _____ hundredths + _____ thousandths

3. Exchange 1 tenth for 10 hundredths or 1 hundredth for 10 thousandths.

a) 6 tenths + 0 hundredths = ___5___ tenths + ___10___ hundredths

b) 9 tenths + 0 hundredths = _____ tenths + _____ hundredths

c) 7 hundredths + 2 thousandths = _____ hundredths + _____ thousandth

d) 4 tenths + 7 hundredths = _____ tenths + _____ hundredths

e) 9 hundredths + 1 thousandth = _____ hundredths + _____ thousandths

f) 5 hundredths + 0 thousandths = _____ hundredths + _____ thousandths

BONUS▶ 1 tenth + 0 hundredths + 5 thousandths = ___ tenths + ___ hundredths + __15__ thousandths

4. Write a fraction for each shaded part. Then add the fractions, and shade your answer.

a)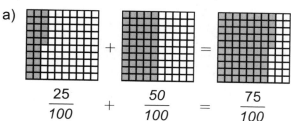

$$\frac{25}{100} + \frac{50}{100} = \frac{75}{100}$$

b)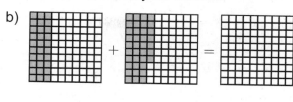

c)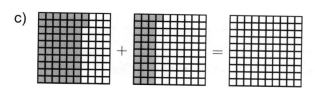

d)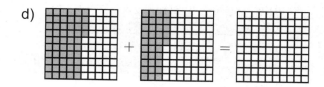

5. Write the decimals that correspond to the fractions in Question 4.

a) .25 + .50 = .75

b) _____

c) _____

d) _____

6. Add by adding each place value.

a) 32.1 + 6.48

Tens	Ones	Tenths	Hundredths
3	2	1	
+	6	4	8
3	8	5	8

b) 40.53 + 27.2

Tens	Ones	Tenths	Hundredths
4	0	5	3
+ 2	7	2	

7. Add by adding each place value and then regroup.

a) 0.72 + 3.5

Ones	Tenths	Hundredths
+		

b) 50.8 + 7.96

Tens	Ones	Tenths	Hundredths
+			

← after regrouping →

8. Add the decimals by lining up the decimal points.

a) 0.32 + 0.57 =

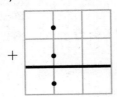

b) 0.91 + 0.04 =

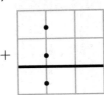

c) 0.5 + 0.48 =

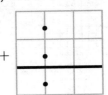

d) 0.22 + 0.57 =

You can show regrouping on a grid. Example: 6.9 + 2.3

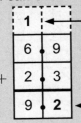

9 tenths + 3 tenths = 12 tenths were regrouped as **1** one and **2** tenths

---

9. Add the decimals by lining up the decimal points. You will need to regroup.

a) 0.8 + 0.56

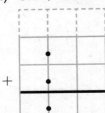

b) 0.37 + 0.48

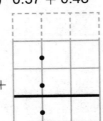

c) 0.81 + 0.58

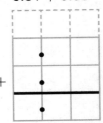

d) 0.46 + 0.22 + 2.37

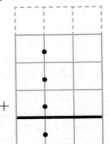

10. Line up the decimal points and add the following numbers.

a) 4.32 + 2.17

b) 3.64 + 5.23

c) 4.872 + 3.191

d) 0.675 + 0.52

11. a) Add .65 + .2 by changing the decimals to fractions:

$$.65 + .2 = \frac{}{100} + \frac{}{10}$$

$$= \frac{}{100} + \frac{}{100}$$

$$= \underline{}$$

b) Add .65 + .2 by lining up the decimal points.

c) Did you get the same answer both ways? If not, find your mistake.

12. Anne made punch by mixing .63 L of juice with .36 L of ginger ale. How many liters of punch did she make?

13. Each wing of a butterfly is 3.72 cm wide. Its body is .46 cm wide. How wide is the butterfly?

14. Subtract by crossing out the correct number of boxes.

a)

$$\frac{50}{100} - \frac{30}{100} =$$

b)

$$\frac{38}{100} - \frac{12}{100} =$$

c)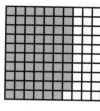

$$\frac{69}{100} - \frac{34}{100} =$$

d)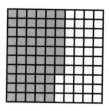

$$\frac{57}{100} - \frac{25}{100} =$$

15. Write the decimals that correspond to the fractions in Question 14.

a) _.50 − .30 = .20_ b) _____ c) _____ d) _____

16. Subtract the decimals by lining up the decimal points.

a) 0.53 − 0.21

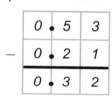

b) 0.88 − 0.34

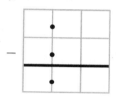

c) 0.46 − 0.23

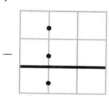

d) 0.75 − 0.21

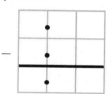

17. Subtract the decimals. You will need to regroup.

a) 0.35 − 0.17

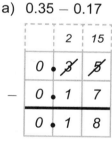

b) 0.64 − 0.38

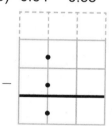

c) 0.92 − 0.59

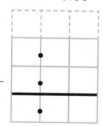

d) 0.53 − 0.26

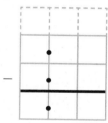

e) 1.00 − .82 f) 1.00 − 0.36 g) 1.00 − 0.44 h) 1.00 − 0.29

18. Subtract the decimals.

a) .82 − .45 b) .97 − .38 c) .72 − .64 d) .31 − .17

e) .58 − .3 f) .62 − .6 g) .987 − .125 h) .530 − .172

19. Find the missing decimal.

a) $1 = .35 +$ [ ] b) $1 = .72 +$ [ ] c) $1 = .41 +$ [ ] d) $1 = .07 +$ [ ]

30. Fractions of a Whole Number

There are 3 equal groups of dots, so each group is $\frac{1}{3}$ of 6.

There are 2 dots in each group, so $\frac{1}{3}$ of 6 is 2.

There are 4 dots in two groups, so $\frac{2}{3}$ of 6 is 4.

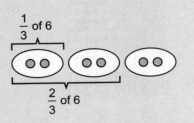

1. Write a fraction for the amount of dots shown.

   a)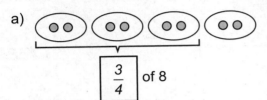

   $\boxed{\frac{3}{4}}$ of 8

   b)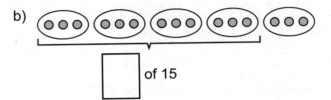

   $\boxed{}$ of 15

2. Fill in the missing numbers.

   a) $\boxed{\frac{1}{3}}$ of 6 = _____

   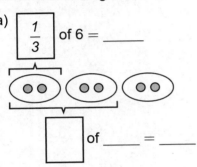

   $\boxed{}$ of ____ = ____

   b) $\boxed{}$ of 8 = _____

   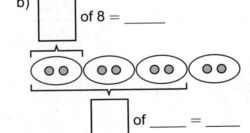

   $\boxed{}$ of ____ = ____

   c) $\boxed{}$ of 9 = _____

   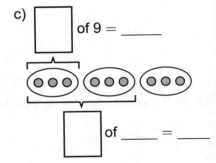

   $\boxed{}$ of ____ = ____

   d)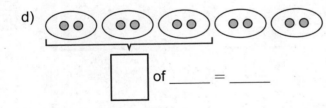

   $\boxed{}$ of ____ = ____

   e)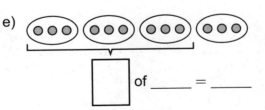

   $\boxed{}$ of ____ = ____

3. Circle the given amount.

   a) $\frac{2}{3}$ of 6

   b) $\frac{3}{4}$ of 8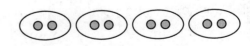

4. Draw the correct number of dots in each group, then circle the given amount.

   a) $\frac{3}{4}$ of 16

   b) $\frac{2}{3}$ of 15

5. Find the fraction of the whole amount by drawing the correct number of groups and then filling in the correct number of dots in each group.

a) $\frac{2}{3}$ of 9 is _____.

b) $\frac{3}{5}$ of 10 is _____.

Andy finds $\frac{2}{3}$ of 12 as follows:

Step 1: He finds $\frac{1}{3}$ of 12 by dividing 12 by 3.

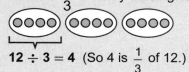

$12 \div 3 = 4$ (So 4 is $\frac{1}{3}$ of 12.)

Step 2: Then he multiplies the result by 2:

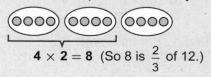

$4 \times 2 = 8$ (So 8 is $\frac{2}{3}$ of 12.)

---

6. Find the following amounts using Andy's method.

a) $\frac{1}{3}$ of 9 = _____ so $\frac{2}{3}$ of 9 = _____

b) $\frac{1}{4}$ of 8 = _____ so $\frac{3}{4}$ of 8 = _____

c) $\frac{1}{3}$ of 15 = _____ so $\frac{2}{3}$ of 15 = _____

d) $\frac{1}{5}$ of 25 = _____ so $\frac{3}{5}$ of 25 = _____

e) $\frac{1}{5}$ of 20 = _____ so $\frac{2}{5}$ of 20 = _____

f) $\frac{1}{7}$ of 21 = _____ so $\frac{3}{7}$ of 21 = _____

7. Twenty students are on a bus. $\frac{3}{5}$ are boys. How many boys are on the bus? _____

8. A store had 15 watermelons. They sold $\frac{2}{3}$ of the watermelons. How many watermelons were sold? _____ How many were left? _____

9. Shade $\frac{1}{4}$ of the squares. Draw stripes in $\frac{1}{6}$ of the squares. How many squares are blank? _____

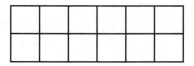

10. Alan started studying at 8:15. He studied history for $\frac{1}{3}$ of an hour and math for $\frac{2}{5}$ of an hour. At what time did he stop studying?

11. Ed has 20 sea shells: $\frac{2}{5}$ are turret shells, $\frac{1}{4}$ are scallops, the rest are conchs. How many shells are conchs?

12. Which is longer, 21 months or $1\frac{5}{6}$ of a year?

BONUS▶ There were 108 grapes. Sara ate $\frac{1}{2}$ of them, Jeff ate $\frac{1}{3}$ of them, and Ron ate $\frac{1}{6}$ of them. How many were left over?

31. Multiplying Fractions by Whole Numbers

REMINDER ▶ Multiplication is a short form for addition.

$3 \times 4 = 4 + 4 + 4$ $5 \times 7 = 7 + 7 + 7 + 7 + 7$ $2 \times 9 = 9 + 9$

1. Write the product as a sum.

a) $3 \times \dfrac{1}{4} = \dfrac{1}{4} + \dfrac{1}{4} + \dfrac{1}{4}$ b) $2 \times \dfrac{3}{7} =$ c) $4 \times \dfrac{5}{11} =$

2. Write the sum as a product.

a) $\dfrac{1}{2} + \dfrac{1}{2} + \dfrac{1}{2} =$ b) $\dfrac{5}{9} + \dfrac{5}{9} =$ c) $\dfrac{3}{4} + \dfrac{3}{4} + \dfrac{3}{4} + \dfrac{3}{4} + \dfrac{3}{4} =$

3. Find the product by first writing it as a sum.

a) $4 \times \dfrac{3}{5} = \dfrac{3}{5} + \dfrac{3}{5} + \dfrac{3}{5} + \dfrac{3}{5} = \dfrac{12}{5}$ b) $2 \times \dfrac{4}{7} =$

c) $6 \times \dfrac{4}{11} =$ d) $5 \times \dfrac{3}{7} =$

To multiply a fraction by a whole number, multiply the numerator by the whole number and leave the denominator the same. Example: $3 \times \dfrac{2}{9} = \dfrac{2}{9} + \dfrac{2}{9} + \dfrac{2}{9}$

$$= \dfrac{2 + 2 + 2}{9}$$

$$= \dfrac{6}{9} \longleftarrow 3 \times 2$$

4. Multiply the fraction by the whole number. Write your answer as a mixed number.

a) $4 \times \dfrac{3}{7} = \dfrac{12}{7} = 1\dfrac{5}{7}$ b) $3 \times \dfrac{4}{5} = \dfrac{}{5} =$ c) $2 \times \dfrac{7}{10} = \dfrac{}{10} =$

d) $7 \times \dfrac{3}{8} = \dfrac{}{8} =$ e) $5 \times \dfrac{2}{3} = \dfrac{}{3} =$ f) $6 \times \dfrac{3}{7} = \dfrac{}{7} =$

5. Find the product. Simplify your answer. (Show your work in your notebook.)

a) $3 \times \dfrac{4}{6} = \dfrac{12}{6} = 2 \longleftarrow 12 \div 6$ b) $8 \times \dfrac{3}{4} =$ c) $5 \times \dfrac{4}{10} =$

d) $12 \times \dfrac{2}{8} =$ e) $3 \times \dfrac{6}{9} =$ f) $7 \times \dfrac{4}{7} =$

g) $9 \times \dfrac{2}{3} =$ h) $12 \times \dfrac{5}{6} =$ i) $15 \times \dfrac{6}{10} =$

JUMP Math Accumula

In mathematics, the word "of" can mean multiply. Examples:

"2 groups of 4" means $2 \times 4 = 8$

2 groups of 4   a group of 8

"$\frac{1}{2}$ of a group of 6" means $\frac{1}{2} \times 6 = 6 \div 2 = 3$

a group of 6

$\frac{1}{2}$ of 6

You can use Andy's method from the previous lesson to multiply a fraction by a whole number.

6. Calculate the product by calculating the fraction of the whole number.

a) $\frac{2}{3} \times 9 = \frac{2}{3}$ of $9 = \underline{\ 6\ } \leftarrow 2 \times (9 \div 3)$

b) $\frac{1}{2} \times 8 = \frac{1}{2}$ of $8 = \underline{\hspace{2cm}}$

c) $\frac{3}{5} \times 10 = \underline{\hspace{2cm}}$

d) $\frac{1}{4} \times 20 = \underline{\hspace{2cm}}$

e) $\frac{5}{6} \times 12 = \underline{\hspace{2cm}}$

f) $\frac{3}{4} \times 16 = \underline{\hspace{2cm}}$

Sohrab and Julie multiply the same numbers, but in a different order.

Sohrab: $\frac{2}{3} \times 6 = 2 \times (6 \div 3)$

$= 2 \times 2$

$= 4$

Julie: $6 \times \frac{2}{3} = (6 \times 2) \div 3$

$= 12 \div 3$

$= 4$

They get the same answer, 4.

7. a) Multiply the same numbers, but in a different order.

i) $\frac{2}{3} \times 9$ and $9 \times \frac{2}{3}$

$= 2 \times (9 \div 3)$ $= (9 \times 2) \div 3$

$=$ $=$

$=$ $=$

ii) $\frac{3}{5} \times 10$ and $10 \times \frac{3}{5}$

$=$ $=$

$=$ $=$

$=$ $=$

iii) $\frac{1}{4} \times 8$ and $8 \times \frac{1}{4}$

iv) $\frac{5}{6} \times 12$ and $12 \times \frac{5}{6}$

b) Do both products have the same answer? If not, find your mistake.

8. To make 1 pie, a recipe calls for $\frac{3}{4}$ of a cup of blueberries.

How many cups of blueberries are needed for 4 pies?

9. Diba's exercise routine takes $\frac{3}{5}$ of an hour. She exercises 5 days a week.

How many hours a week does she exercise?

32. Multiplying Decimals by Powers of 10

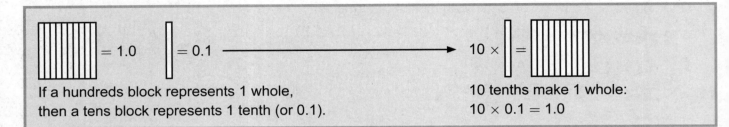

If a hundreds block represents 1 whole,
then a tens block represents 1 tenth (or 0.1).

10 tenths make 1 whole:
$10 \times 0.1 = 1.0$

1. Multiply the number of tens blocks by 10. Draw the number of hundreds blocks you would have, then complete the multiplication sentence.

a)
$10 \times$ [blocks] =

$10 \times 0.2 = \underline{\ 2\ }$

b)
$10 \times$ [blocks] =

$10 \times 0.3 = \underline{\hspace{1cm}}$

c)
$10 \times$ [blocks] =

$10 \times 0.6 = \underline{\hspace{1cm}}$

REMINDER ▶

$\overset{\times\,10}{\frown}$ $\overset{\times\,10}{\frown}$ $\overset{\times\,10}{\frown}$ $\overset{\times\,10}{\frown}$

hundreds ◀ tens ◀ ones ◀ tenths ◀ hundredths

2. Use place value to multiply by 10.

a) 5 hundredths $\times$ 10 = _5 tenths_

b) 7 tenths $\times$ 10 = _____

c) 8 ones $\times$ 10 = _____

d) 3 hundredths $\times$ 10 = _____

e) 9 tenths $\times$ 10 = _____

f) 8 hundredths $\times$ 10 = _____

3. Use place value to multiply by 10.

	Tens	Ones	Tenths	Hundredths
0.04 =			0	4
0.04 × 10 =		0	4	
0.5 =				
0.5 × 10 =				
2.37 =				
2.37 × 10 =				

4. Multiply by 10.

a) $0.5 \times 10 =$ _____   b) $0.08 \times 10 =$ _____   c) $0.003 \times 10 =$ _____   d) $0.6 \times 10 =$ _____

e) $0.07 \times 10 =$ _____   f) $0.004 \times 10 =$ _____   g) $0.2 \times 10 =$ _____   h) $0.09 \times 10 =$ _____

5. Write the number in expanded form, then multiply by 10.

a) $34.5 =$ *30 + 4 + 0.5*   b) $7.12 =$ _____

     So $34.5 \times 10 =$ *300 + 40 + 5*   So $7.12 \times 10 =$ _____

            $=$ *345* $=$ _____

c) $80.04 =$ _____   d) $70.36 =$ _____

     So $80.04 \times 10 =$ _____   So $70.36 \times 10 =$ _____

            $=$ _____ $=$ _____

6. To multiply by 10, shift the decimal point one place to the right.

a) $10 \times 1.7 =$ _____   b) $1.6 \times 10 =$ _____   c) $18.2 \times 10 =$ _____   d) $17.3 \times 10 =$ _____

e) $10 \times 23.5 =$ _____   f) $10 \times 1.72 =$ _____   g) $10 \times 42.6 =$ _____   h) $5.36 \times 10 =$ _____

7. 10×3 can be written as a sum: $3 + 3 + 3 + 3 + 3 + 3 + 3 + 3 + 3 + 3$.
Write 10×0.3 as a sum and skip count by 0.3 to find the answer.

 $= 1.0$ $\square = 0.01$ ——————————————————▶ $100 \times \square =$

If a hundreds block represents 1 whole,
then a ones block represents 1 hundredth (or 0.01).

100 hundredths make 1 whole:
$100 \times 0.01 = 1.0$

8. Write a multiplication equation for the picture.

a)

$100 \times \square =$ [two hundreds blocks]

   100×0.02 $=$ _____

b)

$100 \times \square =$ [three hundreds blocks]

_____ $=$ _____

c)

$100 \times \square =$ [five hundreds blocks]

_____ $=$ _____

> **REMINDER** ▶ Each place value is 100 times greater than the place value two positions over.
>
> Example: 1 thousandth × 100 = 1 tenth, so 0.001 × 100 = 0.1
>
> hundreds   tens   ones   tenths   hundredths   thousandths

9. Multiply the place value by 100.

a) 100 × 1 tenth = *1 ten*   b) 100 × 1 one   c) 100 × 1 hundredth   d) 100 × 1 thousandth

10. Use place value to multiply by 100.

a) 8 thousandths × 100 = ___*8 tenths*___   b) 9 ones × 100 = _____

c) 7 tenths × 100 = _____   d) 6 hundredths × 100 = _____

so 0.7 × 100 = _____   so 0.06 × 100 = _____

11. Write the number in expanded form, then multiply by 100.

a)   3.45 = ___*3 + 0.4 + 0.05*___   b) 80.04 × 100   c) 70.006 × 100

so 3.45 × 100 = ___*300 + 40 + 5 = 345*___   d) 20.3 × 100   e) 2.03 × 100

12. To multiply by 100 or 1,000, shift the decimal point two or three places to the right.

a) 1.7 × 100

I move the decimal point _____ places right.

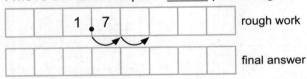

rough work

final answer

b) 1,000 × 0.83

I move the decimal point _____ places right.

rough work

final answer

c) 12.0408 × 1,000

I move the decimal point _____ places right.

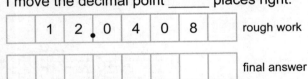

rough work

final answer

d) 100 × 0.95

I move the decimal point _____ places right.

rough work

final answer

13. a) Multiply the fraction by 10. Write your answer in lowest terms.

i) $10 \times \dfrac{2}{10}$ ii) $10 \times \dfrac{3}{100}$ iii) $10 \times \dfrac{16}{10}$ iv) $10 \times \dfrac{5}{1,000}$

b) Multiply the decimal by 10.

i) 10 × 0.2   ii) 10 × 0.03   iii) 10 × 1.6   iv) 10 × 0.005

c) Are your answers to parts a) and b) the same? Why is this the case?

33. Multiplying and Dividing by Powers of 10

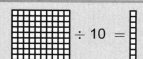 ÷ 10 = │

Divide 1 whole into 10 equal parts; each part is 1 tenth.
1.0 ÷ 10 = 0.1

│ ÷ 10 = ▢

Divide 1 tenth into 10 equal parts; each part is 1 hundredth.
0.1 ÷ 10 = 0.01

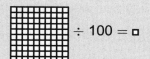 ÷ 100 = ▢

Divide 1 whole into 100 equal parts; each part is 1 hundredth.
1.0 ÷ 100 = 0.01

1. Complete the picture and write a division equation.

a) 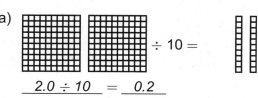 ÷ 10 =

_2.0 ÷ 10_ = _0.2_

b) 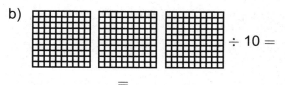 ÷ 10 =

_____ = _____

c) 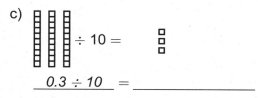 ÷ 10 =

_0.3 ÷ 10_ = _____

d) 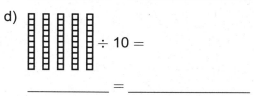 ÷ 10 =

_____ = _____

e) 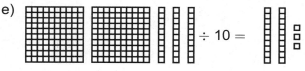 ÷ 10 =

_____ = _____

f) 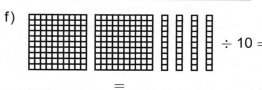 ÷ 10 =

_____ = _____

To divide by 10, 100, or 1,000, shift the decimal point one, two, or three places to the left.

3.84 × 10 = 38.4

2.87 × 100 = 287

0.0352 × 1,000 = 35.2

38.4 ÷ 10 = 3.84

287 ÷ 100 = 2.87

35.2 ÷ 1,000 = 0.0352

---

2. Shift the decimal point one or two places to the left by drawing an arrow, as shown in the box.
Hint: If there is no decimal point, add one to the right of the number first.

a) 0.3 ÷ 10 = _.03_   b) 0.5 ÷ 10 = _____   c) 0.7 ÷ 10 = _____   d) 1.3 ÷ 10 = _____

e) 7.6 ÷ 10 = _____   f) 12.0 ÷ 10 = _____   g) .9 ÷ 10 = _____   h) 27.3 ÷ 10 = _____

i) 3.0 ÷ 100 = _____   j) 6 ÷ 100 = _____   k) .7 ÷ 100 = _____   l) 17.2 ÷ 100 = _____

3. Explain why 1.00 ÷ 100 = .01 using dollar bills as wholes.

4. A wall 3.5 m wide is painted with 100 stripes of equal width. How wide is each stripe?

5. 5 × 3 = 15 and 15 ÷ 5 = 3 are in the same fact family.
Write a division equation in the same fact family as 10 × 0.1 = 1.0.

6. a) To multiply by 10, I move the decimal point __1__ place(s) to the _____right_____ .

   b) To multiply by 1,000, I move the decimal point _____ place(s) to the _____ .

   c) To divide by 100, I move the decimal point _____ place(s) to the _____ .

   d) To divide by 10, I move the decimal point _____ place(s) to the _____ .

   e) To _____ by 1,000, I move the decimal point _____ places to the left.

   f) To _____ by 10, I move the decimal point _____ place to the left.

   g) To _____ by 100, I move the decimal point _____ places to the right.

   h) To divide by 10,000,000, I move the decimal point _____ places to the _____ .

   i) To multiply by 100,000, I move the decimal point _____ places to the _____ .

7. Fill in the blanks. Next, draw arrows to show how you would shift the decimal point.
   Then write your final answer in the grid.

   a) 7.325 × 100

   Move the decimal point __2__ places __right__ .

   | | | 7 . | 3 | 2 | 5 | | rough work |
   | | | 7 | 3 | 2 . | 5 | | final answer |

   b) 5.3 ÷ 1,000

   Move the decimal point __3__ places __left__ .

   | | | | | 5 . | 3 | | | rough work |
   | | | . | 0 | 0 | 5 | 3 | | final answer |

   c) 247.567 × 1,000

   Move the decimal point ____ places _____ .

   | | 2 | 4 | 7 . | 5 | 6 | 7 | | rough work |
   | | | | | | | | | final answer |

   d) 100.45 ÷ 100

   Move the decimal point ____ places _____ .

   | | 1 | 0 | 0 . | 4 | 5 | | | rough work |
   | | | | | | | | | final answer |

   e) 0.602 × 10,000

   Move the decimal point ____ places _____ .

   | | | | . | 6 | 0 | 2 | | rough work |
   | | | | | | | | | final answer |

   f) 24.682 ÷ 10,000

   Move the decimal point ____ places _____ .

   | | | 2 | 4 . | 6 | 8 | 2 | | rough work |
   | | | | | | | | | final answer |

8. Copy the numbers onto grid paper. Show how you would shift the decimal point
   in each case.

   a) 2.65 × 1,000   b) 47.001 × 100   c) 0.043 × 10   d) 20.06 × 1,000   e) 0.07 × 10,000

   f) 0.643 ÷ 10   g) 170.45 ÷ 100   h) 36.07 ÷ 1,000   i) 17.35 ÷ 10,000   j) 0.05 ÷ 1,000

34. Multiplying Decimals by Whole Numbers

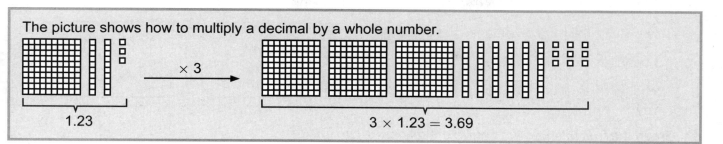

The picture shows how to multiply a decimal by a whole number.

× 3

1.23

3 × 1.23 = 3.69

1. Multiply mentally. Multiply each digit separately.

   a) 3 × 1.32 = _____   b) 2 × 2.4 = _____   c) 6 × 1.01 = _____   d) 3 × 3.2 = _____

   e) 4 × 2.12 = _____   f) 5 × 3.1 = _____   g) 2 × 4.21 = _____   h) 7 × 4.11 = _____

2. Multiply by exchanging tenths for ones.

   a) 7 × 1.3 = __7__ ones + __21__ tenths = __9__ ones + __1__ tenth = __9.1__

   b) 3 × 3.4 = _____ ones + _____ tenths = _____ ones + _____ tenths = _____

   c) 4 × 4.7 = _____ ones + _____ tenths = _____ ones + _____ tenths = _____

   d) 3 × 2.9 = _____

3. Multiply by exchanging tenths for ones or hundredths for tenths.

   a) 3 × 3.51   = __9__ ones + __15__ tenths + __3__ hundredths

                 = _____ ones + _____ tenths + _____ hundredths = _____

   b) 4 × 2.14   = _____ ones + _____ tenths + _____ hundredths

                 = _____ ones + _____ tenths + _____ hundredths = _____

4. Multiply. In some questions you will have to regroup twice.

   a)   b)   c)   d)

   | 2 . 4 | 2 | | 6 . 3 | 5 | | 7 . 2 | 1 | | 2 . 0 | 9 |
   | × | 4 | | × | 3 | | × | 6 | | × | 3 |

5. Find the product.

   a) 5 × 3.6   b) 3 × 0.4   c) 6 × 4.2   d) 9 × 2.27   e) 7 × 34.6   f) 8 × 4.3

   g) 4 × 2.7   h) 5 × 9.52   i) 7 × 5.98   j) 8 × 6.29   k) 3 × 46.92   l) 4 × 36.75

6. You can rewrite the product 80 × 3.6 as 10 × 8 × 3.6. Use this method to find these products.

   a) 40 × 2.1   b) 60 × 0.7   c) 30 × 9.68   d) 200 × 7.5   e) 500 × 0.2

35. Equivalent Ratios

In this picture, the ratio of bananas to apples is

  3 bananas to every 4 apples, **3 : 4** OR

  6 bananas to every 8 apples, **6 : 8**.

1. Group the fruit to show two equivalent ratios.

    a)

    _____ to every _____

    or _____ to every _____

    b)

    _____ to every _____

    or _____ to every _____

2. a) Talia created a sequence of equivalent ratios. She started with the ratio
        2 triangles to every 3 rectangles. Fill in the missing figures and ratios.

Triangles	△ △	△ △ △ △	△ △ △ △ △ △	
Rectangles	▭ ▭ ▭	▭ ▭ ▭ ▭ ▭ ▭		▭ ▭ ▭ ▭ ▭ ▭ ▭ ▭ ▭ ▭ ▭ ▭
Ratio	2 : 3	4 : 6		

    b) Talia records the equivalent ratios in a table.
        Fill in the missing ratios.

        Is this a ratio table? _____ Explain how you know.

        _____

        _____

Triangles	Rectangles
2	3

3. Fill in the ratio table. Then write a sequence of four equivalent ratios.

    a)

3	4
6	8

    b)

2	5

    3 : 4 = _6_ : _8_ = ___ : ___ = ___ : ___

    2 : 5 = _____ = _____ = _____

4. Find the missing term(s).

    a) 3 : 7 = _____ : 14

    b) 5 : 6 = 10 : _____ = _____ : 18   c) 2 : 5 = _____ : 20

36. Finding Equivalent Ratios

A recipe for granola calls for 2 cups of raisins for every 3 cups of oats.

How many cups of raisins will Eschi need for 12 cups of oats?

She writes a sequence of equivalent ratios to find out.

She multiplies both terms in the ratio 2 : 3 by 2, then by 3, then by 4.

2 : 3 = 4 : 6 = 6 : 9 = 8 : 12

Eschi needs 8 cups of raisins.

1. Solve the problem by writing a sequence of equivalent ratios.
   The first one is started for you.

   a) A recipe calls for 5 cups of oats for every 3 cups of raisins.
      How many cups of oats are needed for 12 cups of raisins?

      $5 : 3 = 10 : 6 = \underline{\quad} : \underline{\quad} = \underline{\quad} : \underline{\quad}$

   b) Two centimeters represent 11 km.
      How many kilometers does 8 cm on the map represent?

      _____

   c) Six bus tickets cost $5.
      How much will 18 tickets cost?

      _____

   d) There are 3 red fish for every 5 blue fish in an aquarium.
      If there are 24 red fish, how many blue fish are there?

      _____

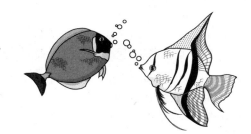

2. Find the missing number in the ratio table.
   Hint: You can use skip counting or multiplication.

   a)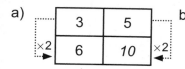

3	5
6	10

   b)

3	4
15	

   c)

3	2
	6

   d)

4	5
20	

   e)

4	9
24	

   f)

6	2
	6

   g)

3	2
27	

   h)

5	2
15	

   Sometimes, the arrow may point from bottom to top.

   i)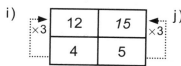

12	15
4	5

   j)

12	
4	9

   k)

	8
3	2

   l)

3	7
12	

m)

	20
7	5

n)

15	
3	8

o)

5	1
	5

p)

8	
4	5

Three subway tickets cost $5. Kyle wants to know how many tickets he can buy for $20. He finds an equivalent ratio using a ratio table:

Step 1: He makes a ratio table showing the cost for each amount of tickets. He writes a question mark (?) for the missing number.

Tickets	Costs ($)
3	5
?	20

Step 2: He finds the number being multiplied by in the second column. Then he multiplies by that number in the first column to find the missing number.

Tickets	Costs ($)
3	5
12	20

×4 ... ×4

Therefore 3 : 5 = 12 : 20 and 12 tickets cost $20.

Use ratio tables to solve the following questions.

3. There are 2 apples in a bowl for every 3 oranges.
If there are 9 oranges, how many apples are there?

4. Five bus tickets cost $3.
How many bus tickets can you buy with $9?

5. To make fruit punch, you mix 1 liter of orange juice with 2 liters of pineapple juice.
If you have 3 liters of orange juice, how many liters of pineapple juice do you need?

6. Nora can run 3 laps in 4 minutes.
At that rate, how many laps could she run in 12 minutes?

7. A basketball team won 2 out of every 3 games they played.
The team played a total of 15 games.
How many games did the team win?
Hint: The quantities are "games won" and "games played."

8. The ratio of boys to girls in a class is 4 : 5.
If there are 20 boys, how many girls are there?

9. Two centimeters on a map represents 5 km in real life.
If a lake is 6 cm long on the map, what is its actual size?

10. In a pet shop, there are 3 cats for every 2 dogs.
If there are 12 cats in the shop,
how many dogs are there?

37. Percentages

> A **percentage** is a ratio that compares a number to 100.
>
> The term percentage means "per 100" or "for every 100" or "out of 100." For example, 84% on a test means 84 out of 100.
>
> You can think of a percentage as a short form for a fraction with denominator 100. Example: $45\% = \dfrac{45}{100}$

1. Write the percentage as a fraction.

   a) 7%   b) 92%   c) 5%   d) 15%

   e) 50%   f) 100%   g) 2%   h) 17%

2. Write the fraction as a percentage.

   a) $\dfrac{2}{100}$ b) $\dfrac{31}{100}$ c) $\dfrac{52}{100}$ d) $\dfrac{100}{100}$

   e) $\dfrac{17}{100}$ f) $\dfrac{88}{100}$ g) $\dfrac{7}{100}$ h) $\dfrac{1}{100}$

3. Write the decimal as a fraction and then a percentage.

   a) $0.72 = \dfrac{72}{100} = 72\%$ b) $0.27 =$ c) $0.04 =$

4. Write the fraction as a percentage by first changing it to a fraction over 100.

   a) $\dfrac{3 \times 20}{5 \times 20} = \dfrac{60}{100} = 60\%$ b) $\dfrac{2}{5}$

   c) $\dfrac{4}{5}$ d) $\dfrac{1}{4}$

   e) $\dfrac{3}{4}$ f) $\dfrac{1}{2}$

   g) $\dfrac{3}{10}$ h) $\dfrac{7}{10}$

   i) $\dfrac{17}{25}$ j) $\dfrac{17}{20}$

   k) $\dfrac{3}{25}$ l) $\dfrac{19}{20}$

   m) $\dfrac{23}{50}$ n) $\dfrac{47}{50}$

5. Write the decimal as a percentage.

a) $0.2 = \dfrac{2 \times 10}{10 \times 10} = \dfrac{20}{100} = 20\%$

b) 0.5

c) 0.7

d) 0.9

6. What percentage of the figure is shaded?

a)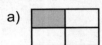

b)

c)

d)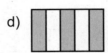

7. Change the fraction to a percentage by first reducing it to lowest terms.

a) $\dfrac{9 \div 3}{15 \div 3} = \dfrac{3}{5} = \dfrac{3 \times 20}{5 \times 20} = \dfrac{60}{100} = 60\%$

b) $\dfrac{12}{15}$

c) $\dfrac{3}{6}$

d) $\dfrac{7}{35}$

e) $\dfrac{21}{28}$

f) $\dfrac{1}{2}$

g) $\dfrac{12}{30}$

h) $\dfrac{10}{40}$

i) $\dfrac{20}{40}$

j) $\dfrac{16}{40}$

k) $\dfrac{60}{150}$

l) $\dfrac{45}{75}$

38. Visual Representations of Percentages

1. Fill in the chart. The first column has been done for you.

Drawing				
Fraction	$\frac{23}{100}$	$\frac{}{100}$	$\frac{45}{100}$	$\frac{}{100}$
Decimal	0.23	0.____	0.____	0.81
Percentage	23%	63%	____%	____%

Use a ruler for Questions 2–4.

2. Shade 50% of the shape.

a)

b)

c)

3. Shade 25% of the box.

a)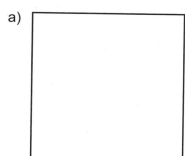

b)

c)

4. Color 50% of the rectangle blue, 40% red, and 10% green.

5. a) Write a fraction for the shaded part: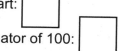

   b) Write the fraction with a denominator of 100:

   c) Write a decimal and percentage for the shaded part: _____ _____

6. Write a fraction and a percentage for each division of the number line.

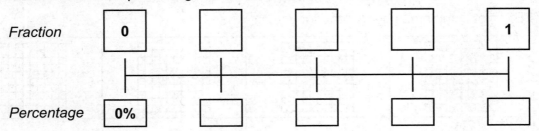

Fraction | 0 | | | | 1

Percentage | 0% | | | |

7. Draw marks to show 25%, 50%, and 75% of the line segment.

a) ————|——|——|————

b) ——————————————————

c) ————————————

d) ——————————————————————

8. Extend the line segment to show 100%.

a) |—— 50% ——|————————|

b) |— 25% —|

c) |20%|

d) |———— 75% ————|

e) |————————————|
    0%   60%

f) |————————————|
    0%   80%

g) |———|
    0% 10%

9. Estimate the percentage of the line segment to the left of the mark.

a) |————————✕————|
    0%   100%

b) |————✕————————|
    0%   100%

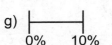**10.** Draw a rough sketch of a floor plan for a museum.

The different collections should take up the following amounts of space:

- Dinosaurs   40%
- Animals   20%
- Rocks and Minerals   10%
- Ancient Artifacts   20%

Washrooms should take up the final 10% of the floor space.

11. Asia covers 30% of the world's landmass.
Using a globe, compare the size of Asia to the size of Australia.
Approximately what percentage of the world's landmass does Australia cover?

JUMP Math Accumula

39. Comparing Decimals, Fractions, and Percentages

1. From the list below, choose the percentage closest to the fraction.

| 10% | 25% | 50% | 75% |

a) $\dfrac{3}{5}$ ____

b) $\dfrac{4}{5}$ ____

c) $\dfrac{2}{5}$ ____

d) $\dfrac{2}{10}$ ____

e) $\dfrac{1}{10}$ ____

f) $\dfrac{4}{10}$ ____

g) $\dfrac{9}{10}$ ____

h) $\dfrac{4}{25}$ ____

i) $\dfrac{11}{20}$ ____

j) $\dfrac{16}{20}$ ____

k) $\dfrac{37}{40}$ ____

l) $\dfrac{1}{12}$ ____

2. Write $<$, $>$, or $=$ between each pair of numbers. Change the numbers in each pair to fractions with the same denominator first.

a) $\dfrac{1}{2}$ ☐ 47%

$\dfrac{50 \times 1}{50 \times 2}$ ☐ $\dfrac{47}{100}$

$\dfrac{50}{100}$ ☐$>$☐ $\dfrac{47}{100}$

b) $\dfrac{1}{2}$ ☐ 53%

☐

☐

c) $\dfrac{1}{4}$ ☐ 23%

☐

☐

d) $\dfrac{3}{4}$ ☐ 70%

☐

☐

e) $\dfrac{2}{5}$ ☐ 32%

☐

☐

f) 0.27 ☐ 62%

☐

☐

g) 0.02 ☐ 11%

☐

☐

h) $\dfrac{1}{10}$ ☐ 10%

☐

☐

i) $\dfrac{19}{25}$ ☐ 93%

☐

☐

j) $\dfrac{23}{50}$ ☐ 46%

☐

☐

k) 0.9 ☐ 10%

☐

☐

l) $\dfrac{11}{20}$ ☐ 19%

☐

☐

3. Write the set of numbers in order from least to greatest by first changing each number to a *fraction*.

a) $\dfrac{3}{5}$, 42% , .73

b) $\dfrac{1}{2}$, .73 , 80%

c) $\dfrac{1}{4}$, .09 , 15%

d) $\dfrac{2}{3}$, 57% , .62

40. Long Multiplication (Review)

To multiply 37 × 20, first multiply 37 × 2, then multiply by 10.
This is how to record your answer on a grid:

1. Multiply.

a)

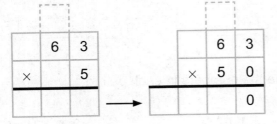

b)

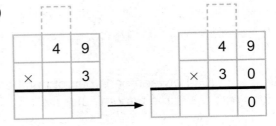

c)

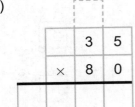

d)

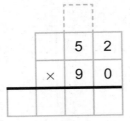

e)

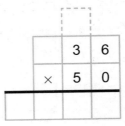

f)

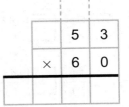

To multiply 37 × 25, split 25 into two numbers that are
easier to multiply by. The picture shows why this works.

a multiple of 10 ⟶   ⟵ a 1-digit number

37 × 25 = 37 × **20** + 37 × **5**

$\quad\quad\quad = 740 + 185$

$\quad\quad\quad = 925$

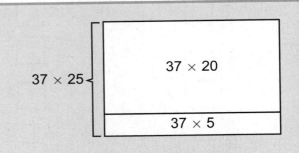

2. Multiply. Do your rough work in your notebook.

a) 34 × 27

34 × 20 = _____

34 × 7 = _____

so 34 × 27 = _____

b) 56 × 32

56 × 30 = _____

56 × 2 = _____

so 56 × 32 = _____

c) 83 × 26

83 × 20 = _____

83 × 6 = _____

so 83 × 26 = _____

d) 78 × 45

78 × 40 = _____

78 × 5 = _____

so 78 × 45 = _____

JUMP Math Accumula

You can record the steps in multiplying 2-digit numbers on a grid.

Example: Find 37 × 25.

Step 1: Calculate 37 × 5.

Step 2: Calculate 37 × 20.

Step 3: Add the results.

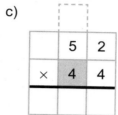

37 × 5

37 × 20

3. Practice Step 1.

a)
	1	
	2	4
×	1	3
	7	2	= 24 × 3

b)
	3	3
×	3	9

c)
	5	2
×	4	4

d)
	1	6
×	3	5

4. Practice Step 2.

a)
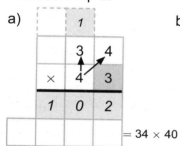
= 34 × 40

b)
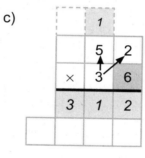

c)
		1	
		5	2
	×	3	6
	3	1	2

d)
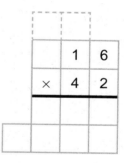

5. Practice Steps 1 and 2.

a)
Regrouping 35 × 20
Regrouping for 35 × 6
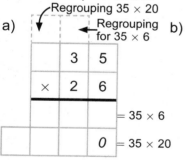
= 35 × 6
= 35 × 20

b)
	3	2
×	5	4

c)
	4	5
×	3	5

d)
	1	6
×	4	2

6. Multiply.

a)
		3	7
	×	2	5
+			0

b)
		6	9
	×	5	3
+			0

c)
		7	4
	×	5	2

d)
		5	4
	×	3	2

41. Finding Percentages

If you use a thousands cube to represent 1 whole, you can see that taking $\frac{1}{10}$ of a number is the same as dividing the number by 10—the decimal shifts one place left.

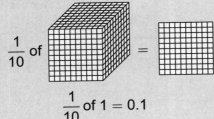

$\frac{1}{10}$ of $\boxed{}$ = $\boxed{}$

$\frac{1}{10}$ of 1 = 0.1 $\frac{1}{10}$ of 0.1 = 0.01 $\frac{1}{10}$ of 0.01 = 0.001

1. Find $\frac{1}{10}$ of the number by shifting the decimal. Write your answer in the box provided.

   a) 4 (= 4.0)   b) 7   c) 32   d) 120   e) 3.8   f) 2.5

   $\boxed{0.4}$ $\boxed{}$ $\boxed{}$ $\boxed{}$ $\boxed{}$ $\boxed{}$

2. 10% is short for $\frac{1}{10}$. Find 10% of the number.

   a) 9   b) 5.7   c) 4.05   d) 6.35   e) 0.06   f) 21.1

   $\boxed{}$ $\boxed{}$ $\boxed{}$ $\boxed{}$ $\boxed{}$ $\boxed{}$

You can find percentages that are multiples of 10.

Example: To find 30% of 21, find 10% of 21 and multiply the result by 3.

Step 1: 10% of 21 = $\boxed{2.1}$

Step 2: 3 × $\boxed{2.1}$ = 6.3 ⟶ 30% of 21 = 6.3

---

3. Find the percentage using the method above.

   a) 40% of 15
      i) 10% of _15_ = $\boxed{}$
      ii) _4_ × $\boxed{}$ = _____

   b) 60% of 25
      i) 10% of _____ = $\boxed{}$
      ii) ___ × $\boxed{}$ = _____

   c) 90% of 2.3
      i) 10% of _____ = $\boxed{}$
      ii) ___ × $\boxed{}$ = _____

   d) 60% of 35
      i) 10% of _____ = $\boxed{}$
      ii) ___ × $\boxed{}$ = _____

   e) 40% of 24
      i) 10% of _____ = $\boxed{}$
      ii) ___ × $\boxed{}$ = _____

   f) 20% of 1.3
      i) 10% of _____ = $\boxed{}$
      ii) ___ × $\boxed{}$ = _____

42. Finding Percentages Using Multiplication

Remember: 35% is short for $\frac{35}{100}$. To find 35% of 27, Sadie finds $\frac{35}{100}$ of 27.

Step 1: She multiplies 27 by 35.   **Step 2:** She divides the result by 100.

$$945 \div 100 = 9.45$$

So 35% of 27 is 9.45.

1. Find the percentage using Sadie's method.

   a) 45% of 32

   Step 1:

   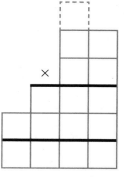

   Step 2:

   _____ ÷ 100 =

   So _____ of _____ is _____ .

   b) 28% of 63

   Step 1:

   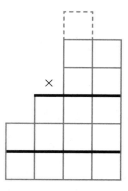

   Step 2:

   _____ ÷ 100 =

   So _____ of _____ is _____ .

2. Find the percentage using Sadie's method.

   a) 13% of 9   b) 52% of 7   c) 65% of 8   d) 78% of 9

   e) 23% of 42   f) 17% of 68   g) 37% of 80   h) 62% of 75

3. 25% is equal to $\frac{1}{4}$ and 75% is equal to $\frac{3}{4}$. Find…

   a) 25% of 80.   b) 25% of 280.   c) 25% of 12.   d) 75% of 20.   e) 75% of 320.

43. Percentages: Word Problems

1. Find the percentage of each child's stamp collection that comes from "other" countries.
   Hint: Change all fractions to percentages.

   a) Anne's collection:

USA	Canada	Other
40%	$\frac{1}{2}$	
= 40%	= 50%	= 10%

   b) Brian's collection:

USA	England	Other
80%	$\frac{1}{10}$	

   c) Juan's collection:

Mexico	USA	Other
$\frac{1}{2}$	40%	

   d) Lanre's collection:

USA	Nigeria	Other
22%	$\frac{3}{5}$	

   e) Faith's collection:

Jamaica	USA	Other
$\frac{3}{4}$	15%	

   f) Carlo's collection:

France	Italy	Other
$\frac{3}{4}$	10%	

2. A painter spends $500.00 on art supplies. Complete the chart.

	Fraction of Money Spent	Percentage of Money Spent	Amount of Money Spent
Brushes			$50.00
Paint	$\frac{4}{10}$		
Canvas		50%	

3. Indra spent 1 hour doing homework. The chart shows the time she spent on each subject.

   a) Complete the chart.

   b) How did you find the amount of time spent on math?

Subject	Fraction of 1 Hour	Percent of 1 Hour	Decimal	Number of Minutes
English	$\frac{1}{4}$		.25	15
Science	$\frac{1}{20}$	5%		
Math		50%		
French			.20	

4. Roger wants to buy a deck of cards that costs $8.00. The taxes are 15%. How much did he pay in taxes?

5. There are 15 boys and 12 girls in a class.
   $\frac{3}{4}$ of the girls have black hair, and 60% of the boys have black hair.
   How many children have black hair?

44. Fractions, Ratios, and Percentages

1. Write the number of boys (**b**), girls (**g**), and children (**c**) in each class.

   a) There are 8 boys and 5 girls in a class.   **b:** _8_   **g:** _5_   **c:** _13_

   b) There are 4 boys and 7 girls in a class.   **b:** _____   **g:** _____   **c:** _____

   c) There are 12 boys and 15 girls in a class.   **b:** _____   **g:** _____   **c:** _____

   d) There are 9 girls in a class of 20 children.   **b:** _____   **g:** _____   **c:** _____

   e) There are 7 boys in a class of 10 children.   **b:** _____   **g:** _____   **c:** _____

2. Write the number of boys, girls, and children in each class.
   Then write the fraction of children who are boys and the fraction who are girls.

   a) There are 5 boys and 6 girls in a class.   **b:** _5_ $\dfrac{5}{11}$ **g:** _6_ $\boxed{}$ **c:** _____

   b) There are 15 children in the class. 8 are boys.   **b:** _____ $\boxed{}$ **g:** _____ $\boxed{}$ **c:** _____

3. Write the fraction of children in the class who are boys and the fraction who are girls.

   a) There are 5 boys and 17 children in the class.   **b:** $\dfrac{5}{17}$ **g:** $\boxed{}$

   b) There are 3 boys and 2 girls in the class.   **b:** $\boxed{}$ **g:** $\boxed{}$

   c) There are 9 girls and 20 children in the class.   **b:** $\boxed{}$ **g:** $\boxed{}$

   d) The ratio of boys to girls in the class is 5 : 9.   **b:** $\boxed{}$ **g:** $\boxed{}$

   e) The ratio of girls to boys in the class is 7 : 8.   **b:** $\boxed{}$ **g:** $\boxed{}$

   f) The ratio of boys to girls in the class is 10 : 11.   **b:** $\boxed{}$ **g:** $\boxed{}$

   g) The ratio of boys to students in the class is 11 : 23.   **b:** $\boxed{}$ **g:** $\boxed{}$

   h) The ratio of students to girls in the class is 25 : 13.   **b:** $\boxed{}$ **g:** $\boxed{}$

4. Fill in the missing numbers for each classroom.

	Ratio of				What Fraction	
	girls to students	boys to students	girls to boys	boys to girls	are girls?	are boys?
a)	2 : 5	3 : 5	2 : 3	3 : 2	$\frac{2}{5}$	$\frac{3}{5}$
b)	4 : 7					
c)						$\frac{1}{4}$
d)		23 : 50				
e)				9 : 16		
f)						$\frac{1}{2}$
g)			7 : 10			
h)					$\frac{12}{15}$	
i)				25 : 31		

5. Fill in the missing numbers for each classroom.

	Percent that Are Girls	Percent that Are Boys	Fraction that Are Girls	Fraction that Are Boys	Ratio of Girls to Boys
a)	40%	60%	$\frac{40}{100}$	$\frac{60}{100}$	40 : 60
b)		35%			
c)				$\frac{3}{4}$	
d)					10 : 15
e)			$\frac{1}{2}$		
f)	65%				
g)					23 : 27

There are 3 boys for every 2 girls in a class of 20 students. How many boys are in the class?

Method 1: Julie writes a sequence of equivalent ratios.

3 boys : 2 girls = 6 boys : 4 girls = 9 boys : 6 girls = 12 boys : 8 girls

There are 12 boys in the class.

Stop when the terms of the ratio add to 20.

Method 2: Sally uses different equivalent ratios to find the answer.
There are 3 boys for every 5 students in the class.

3 boys : 5 students = 6 boys : 10 students = 9 boys : 15 students = 12 boys : 20 students

There are 12 boys in the class.

Stop when you reach 20.

Method 3: Karen uses fractions. The ratio of boys to girls is 3 : 2. $\frac{3}{5} \times 20 = 12$

So the fraction of boys in the class is $\frac{3}{5}$. So there are 12 boys in the class.

6. From the information given, determine the number of girls and boys in each class.

a) There are 20 children in a class. $\frac{2}{5}$ are boys.   b) There are 42 children. $\frac{3}{7}$ are girls.

c) There are 15 children.
The ratio of girls to boys is 3 : 2.

d) There are 24 children.
The ratio of girls to boys is 3 : 5.

7. Which classroom has more girls?

a) In Classroom A, there are 40 children. 60% are girls.

In Classroom B, there are 36 children. The ratio of boys to girls is 5 : 4.

b) In Classroom A, there are 28 children. The ratio of boys to girls is 5 : 2.

In Classroom B, there are 30 children. $\frac{3}{5}$ of the children are boys.

8. Look at the word "California."

a) What is the ratio of vowels to consonants?

b) What fraction of the letters are vowels?

c) What percentage of the letters are consonants?

9. Write the amounts in order from least to greatest: $\frac{1}{20}$, 20% , 0.2. Show your work.

10. Kevin has 360 hockey cards. Thirty percent are New York Rangers cards, and half are Detroit Red Wings cards. The rest are Los Angeles Kings cards. How many cards from each team does Kevin have?

45. Long Division (Review)

Linda needs to divide 95 objects into 4 equal groups.
She uses long division and a model to solve the problem.

$95 = 9$ tens $+ 5$ ones

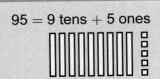

Step 1: Write the numbers like this:

the number of groups ⟶ 4$\overline{)95}$ ⟵ the number of objects to be divided

1. Fill in the blanks for the division expression.

   a) 2$\overline{)53}$ ___ groups ___ tens ___ ones   b) 5$\overline{)71}$ ___ groups ___ tens ___ ones

   c) 4$\overline{)97}$ ___ groups ___ tens ___ ones   d) 5$\overline{)88}$ ___ groups ___ tens ___ ones

Step 2: How many tens can be put in each group?

2 tens in each group ⟶ **2**

4 groups ⟶ 4$\overline{)}$ 9 5

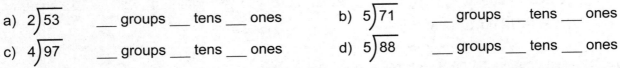

2. How many tens can be put in each group?

   a) 2
       4$\overline{)}$ 8 7

   b) 3$\overline{)}$ 9 4

   c) 6$\overline{)}$ 7 4

   d) 2$\overline{)}$ 9 8

3. For the division expression, write how many groups are being made and how many tens can be put in each group.

   a) 4$\overline{)}$ 5 5

   groups _____

   number of tens
   in each group _____

   b) 5$\overline{)}$ 9 7

   groups _____

   number of tens
   in each group _____

   c) 3$\overline{)}$ 7 6

   groups _____

   number of tens
   in each group _____

   d) 3$\overline{)}$ 8 9

   groups _____

   number of tens
   in each group _____

Step 3: How many tens have been placed in the groups altogether?

× ⟍ **2** ⟵ 2 tens in each group

4 groups ⟶ 4$\overline{)}$ 9 5

8 ⟵ $2 \times 4 = 8$ tens have been placed

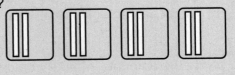

4. Multiply to decide how many tens have been placed altogether.

   a) ×⟍ 2
      3$\overline{)}$ 8 7
         6

   b) 2
      4$\overline{)}$ 9 9

   c) 3
      2$\overline{)}$ 7 9

   d) 4
      2$\overline{)}$ 8 9

5. Use skip counting to find out how many tens can be placed in each group.
Then use multiplication to find out how many tens have been placed altogether.

a)   8)9 4   b)   5)9 4   c)   2)8 8   d)   7)9 5   e)   3)8 7

f)   4)8 5   g)   4)9 2   h)   5)6 3   i)   2)9 8   j)   6)9 0

Step 4: How many tens are left over?

There are 9 tens.

Linda has placed 8.

$9 - 8 = 1$ ten is left over ⟶

```
    2
4)  9  5
  - 8
    1
```

1 ten left over

6. Carry out the first four steps of long division. Use grid paper for parts f) to j).

a)   7)9 7   b)   3)7 4   c)   2)6 3   d)   4)7 3   e)   6)8 9

f) 7)85   g) 7)84   h) 3)87   i) 5)71   j) 4)52

Step 5: There are 1 ten and 5 ones left over.
So there are 15 ones left over.

Write 5 beside the 1 to show this.

```
    2
4)  9  5
  - 8 ↓
    1  5
```

There are 15 ones still to place

7. Carry out the first five steps of long division. Use grid paper for parts f) to j).

a)   5)7 5   b)   7)8 7   c)   4)9 3   d)   2)7 3   e)   2)7 4

f) 8)97   g) 4)76   h) 3)94   i) 7)91   j) 9)94

Step 6: How many ones can be placed in each group?

Divide to find out.

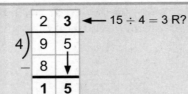

15 ÷ 4 = 3 R?

    ?

How many ones are left over?

8. Carry out the first six steps of long division.

a) 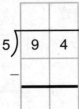 b) 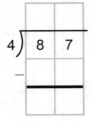 c) 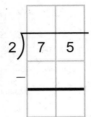 d) 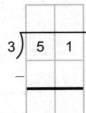 e)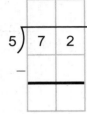

f) 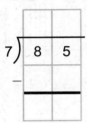 g) 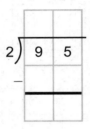 h) 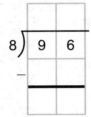 i) 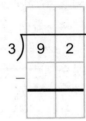 j)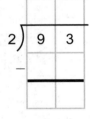

Step 7: How many ones are left over?

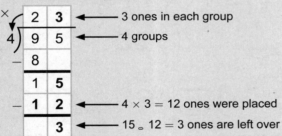

3 ones in each group

4 groups

4 × 3 = 12 ones were placed

15 – 12 = 3 ones are left over

3 ones are left over

95 ÷ 4 = 23 with 3 left over

9. Carry out all seven steps of long division. Use grid paper for parts f) to j).

a)  b) 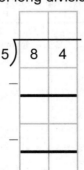 c) 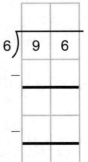 d) 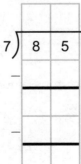 e)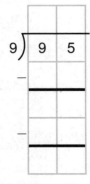

f) 4)65 g) 6)78 h) 3)84 i) 3)75 j) 3)96

JUMP Math Accumula

46. Long Division and Unit Rates

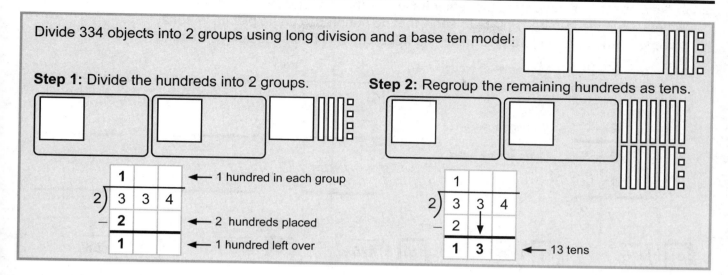

Divide 334 objects into 2 groups using long division and a base ten model:

Step 1: Divide the hundreds into 2 groups.

1 hundred in each group
2 hundreds placed
1 hundred left over

Step 2: Regroup the remaining hundreds as tens.

13 tens

1. Carry out the first two steps of long division.

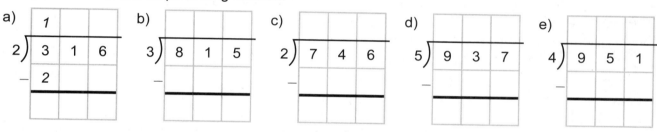

a) 2) 3 1 6 — 2

b) 3) 8 1 5

c) 2) 7 4 6

d) 5) 9 3 7

e) 4) 9 5 1

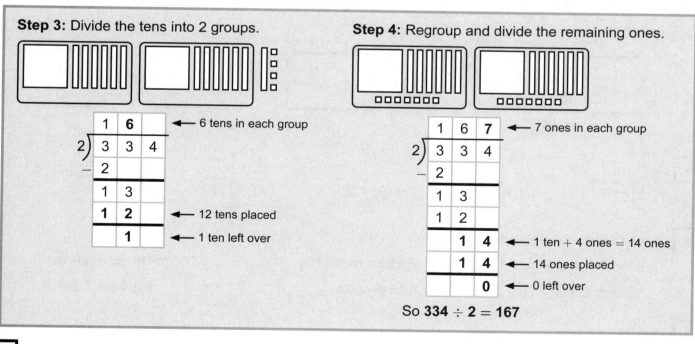

Step 3: Divide the tens into 2 groups.

6 tens in each group
12 tens placed
1 ten left over

Step 4: Regroup and divide the remaining ones.

7 ones in each group
1 ten + 4 ones = 14 ones
14 ones placed
0 left over

So **334 ÷ 2 = 167**

2. Divide. Use grid paper.

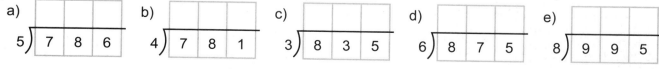

a) 5) 7 8 6

b) 4) 7 8 1

c) 3) 8 3 5

d) 6) 8 7 5

e) 8) 9 9 5

3. In each question below, there are fewer hundreds than the number of groups.
   Write a "0" in the hundreds place to show that no hundreds can be placed in equal
   groups. Then perform the division as if the hundreds had been exchanged for tens.

a)
```
      0   4 ← 3 ── 4 tens in each group
  8) 3   4   6
  -   3   2 ← ──── 32 tens placed
          2 ← 6 ── 2 tens are left over
  -       2   4
              2
```

b)  5) 4 7 5

c) 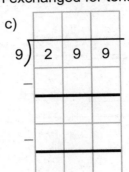 9) 2 9 9

d) 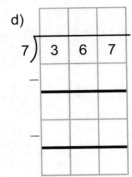 7) 3 6 7

 e) 3) 115   f) 4) 341   g) 8) 425   h) 6) 379   i) 9) 658

4. In each question below, there are not enough tens to divide into the groups.
   Write a "0" in the tens place to show that no tens can be placed, then continue
   the division, regrouping tens as ones.

a)
```
      2   0 ← 8 ── 0 tens in each group
  3) 6   2   5
  -   6
      0   2 ← ──── 2 tens to place in 3 groups
  -       0 ← ──── 0 tens placed
          2   5
  -       2   4
              1
```

b) 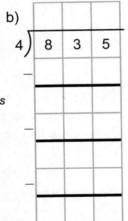 4) 8 3 5

c) 2) 8 1 5

d) 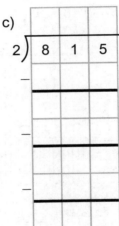 7) 7 5 3

5. Divide.
   a) 3) 417   b) 4) 821   c) 8) 725   d) 6) 973   e) 9) 639

6. Divide to find the missing information.
   a) 5 jackets cost $75   b) 6 tickets cost $138   c) 148 miles per 4 gallons
      1 jacket costs _____   1 ticket costs _____   _____ miles per 1 gallon

7. Find the unit rate.
   a) 3 boxes for 72 cans   b) 236 miles in 4 hours   c) $104 for 8 hours
      1 box for _____ cans   _____ miles in 1 hour   _____ per hour

8. Which is the best deal for renting skates? **A.** $30 for 2 hours, **B.** $48 for 4 hours, or **C.** $39 for 3 hours

JUMP Math Accumula

47. Tape Diagrams

Rita mixes 4 cups of mango juice with 3 cups of orange juice to make fruit punch. She uses a **tape diagram** to represent the mixture:

Mango juice:

Orange juice:

*The total amount of the fruit punch has 7 **equal** parts.*

A tape diagram has two (or more) strips, one on top of the other. The strips are made of units of the same size.

1. Use a tape diagram to represent the number of boys and girls.

a) The ratio of girls to boys is 3 : 2.

girls:

boys:

__3__ girls and

__2__ boys

for every __5__ students

b) The ratio of girls to boys is 2 : 3.

girls:

boys:

____ girls and

____ boys

for every ____ students

c) The ratio of boys to girls is 1 : 3.

girls:

boys:

____ girls and

____ boys

for every ____ students

d) The ratio of girls to boys is 3 : 4.

girls:

boys:

____ girls and

____ boys

for every ____ students

e) $\frac{3}{5}$ are girls.

girls:

boys:

____ girls and

____ boys

for every ____ students

f) $\frac{3}{7}$ are boys.

girls:

boys:

____ girls and

____ boys

for every ____ students

2. Use a tape diagram to represent the number of each part. Sometimes, there are more than two parts in a whole.

a) The ratio of kiwis to limes is 4 : 3.

kiwis:

limes:

____ kiwis and

____ limes

for every ____ fruit

b) $\frac{1}{5}$ of the audience is students.

students:

non-students:

c) There are 3 adults and 2 seniors for each child in the store.

children:

adults:

seniors:

____ child, ____ adults

and ____ seniors

for every ____ people

d) For each cup of orange juice, there are 4 cups of cranberry juice and 2 cups of apple juice.

orange:

cranberry:

apple:

Using the recipe 4 cups of mango juice for 3 cups of orange juice, Rita makes 35 cups of punch in total. Rita uses a tape diagram and ratio tables to find how many cups of each juice she needs.

Step 1: She uses a tape diagram to find the ratio of each part to the whole.

Mango juice: ⬛⬛⬛⬛ *ratio of mango juice to punch is **4** :7*

Orange juice: ⬜⬜⬜ *ratio of orange juice to punch is **3** :7*

Step 2: She uses two ratio tables to find how many cups of each juice.

Cups of Mango	Cups in Total
4	7
20	35

×5 →

Cups of Orange	Cups in Total
3	7
15	35

×5 → ×5

Rita needs to mix 20 cups of mango juice and 15 cups of orange juice to make her punch.

3. Use a tape diagram to find the ratio, and then solve the problem.

   a) In a pet shop, there are 3 cats for every 5 dogs. If there are 40 pets in the shop, how many dogs are there?

   dogs: ⬛⬛⬛⬛⬛ ratio of dogs to pets
   cats: ⬜⬜⬜   is 5 : 8

Dogs	Pets

   b) There are 2 red fish for every 5 blue fish in an aquarium. If there are 21 fish in the aquarium, how many blue fish are in the aquarium?

Blue Fish	Total Fish

   c) There are 35 children in a class. The ratio of girls to boys is 3 : 2. Determine the number of girls and boys in the class.

BONUS ▶ A punch recipe calls for 6 cups of mango juice and 2 cups of orange juice. How many cups of each juice do you need to make 20 cups of punch?

48. Writing Equivalent Statements for Proportions

These are equivalent statements:

$\dfrac{6}{9}$ of the circles are shaded.

6 is $\dfrac{2}{3}$ of 9.

$\dfrac{2}{3}$ of the circles are shaded.

$6 : 9 = 2 : 3$

part   whole

1. Write four equivalent statements for the picture.

a)

$\dfrac{4}{6}$ are shaded

$\dfrac{2}{3}$ are shaded

4 is $\dfrac{2}{3}$ of 6

$4 : 6 = 2 : 3$

b)

c)

d)

2. For the picture, write a pair of equivalent ratios.

a)

4 is $\dfrac{1}{2}$ of 8

$\dfrac{4}{\text{part}} : \dfrac{8}{\text{whole}} = \dfrac{1}{} : \dfrac{2}{}$

b)

6 is $\dfrac{3}{5}$ of 10

$\dfrac{}{\text{part}} : \dfrac{}{\text{whole}} = \underline{\quad} : \underline{\quad}$

c)

2 is $\dfrac{1}{4}$ of 8

$\dfrac{}{\text{part}} : \dfrac{}{\text{whole}} = \underline{\quad} : \underline{\quad}$

3. For the statement, write a pair of equivalent ratios and equivalent fractions.

a) 15 is $\dfrac{3}{4}$ of 20 $\dfrac{}{\text{part}} : \dfrac{}{\text{whole}} = \underline{\quad} : \underline{\quad}$ $\dfrac{\text{part}}{\text{whole}} \quad \underline{\quad} = \underline{\quad}$

b) 18 is $\dfrac{9}{10}$ of 20 $\dfrac{}{\text{part}} : \dfrac{}{\text{whole}} = \underline{\quad} : \underline{\quad}$ $\dfrac{\text{part}}{\text{whole}} \quad \underline{\quad} = \underline{\quad}$

4. Fill in the blanks. Write a question mark where you are missing a piece of information.

a) 12 is $\frac{4}{5}$ of what number? $\underline{\frac{12}{\text{part}}} : \underline{\frac{?}{\text{whole}}} = \underline{4} : \underline{5}$ $\frac{\text{part}}{\text{whole}}$ $\frac{12}{?} = \frac{4}{5}$

b) 6 is how many quarters of 8? $\underline{\frac{6}{\text{part}}} : \underline{\frac{8}{\text{whole}}} = \underline{?} : \underline{4}$ $\frac{\text{part}}{\text{whole}}$ $\underline{\quad} = \underline{\quad}$

c) What is $\frac{3}{4}$ of 16? $\underline{\frac{\quad}{\text{part}}} : \underline{\frac{\quad}{\text{whole}}} = \underline{\quad} : \underline{\quad}$ $\frac{\text{part}}{\text{whole}}$ $\underline{\quad} = \underline{\quad}$

d) 20 is how many thirds of 30? $\underline{\frac{\quad}{\text{part}}} : \underline{\frac{\quad}{\text{whole}}} = \underline{\quad} : \underline{\quad}$ $\frac{\text{part}}{\text{whole}}$ $\underline{\quad} = \underline{\quad}$

5. For the statement, write a pair of equivalent ratios and a pair of equivalent fractions.

a) 15 is what percent of 20? $\underline{\frac{15}{\text{part}}} : \underline{\frac{20}{\text{whole}}} = \underline{?} : \underline{100}$ $\frac{\text{part}}{\text{whole}}$ $\frac{15}{20} = \frac{?}{100}$

b) What is 25% of 80? $\underline{\frac{\quad}{\text{part}}} : \underline{\frac{\quad}{\text{whole}}} = \underline{\quad} : \underline{\quad}$ $\frac{\text{part}}{\text{whole}}$ $\underline{\quad} = \underline{\quad}$

c) 18 is 3% of what number? $\underline{\frac{\quad}{\text{part}}} : \underline{\frac{\quad}{\text{whole}}} = \underline{\quad} : \underline{\quad}$ $\frac{\text{part}}{\text{whole}}$ $\underline{\quad} = \underline{\quad}$

6. Write the two pieces of information you are given and what you need to find (?).
Then write an equation for the problem.

a) What percent of 25 is 5?   part $\underline{5}$ whole $\underline{25}$ percent $\underline{?}$ $\frac{5}{25} = \frac{?}{100}$

b) If 7 is 20%, what is 100%?   part $\underline{\quad}$ whole $\underline{?}$ percent $\underline{\quad}$ $\frac{\quad}{?} = \frac{\quad}{100}$

c) What is 18% of 25?   part $\underline{?}$ whole $\underline{\quad}$ percent $\underline{\quad}$ $\frac{?}{\quad} = \frac{\quad}{100}$

d) If 3 is 12%, what is 100%?   part $\underline{\quad}$ whole $\underline{\quad}$ percent $\underline{\quad}$ $\frac{\quad}{\quad} = \frac{\quad}{100}$

e) What percent of 50 is 4?   part $\underline{\quad}$ whole $\underline{\quad}$ percent $\underline{\quad}$ $\frac{\quad}{\quad} = \frac{\quad}{100}$

Solve the proportion.

$\frac{3}{5} = \frac{?}{100}$

Step 1
Notice: $5 \times 20 = 100$

Step 2
Write what you would multiply by.

$$\frac{3 \xrightarrow{\times 20} ?}{5 \xrightarrow{\times 20} 100}$$

Step 3
$\frac{3}{5} = \frac{60}{100}$

---

7. Solve the proportions in Question 6 using the method above.

49. Solving Equations—Using Logic

To solve the equation $x + 3 = 8$, Mike and Jill use different methods.

Mike uses preserving equality:

$$x + 3 = 8$$
$$x + 3 - 3 = 8 - 3$$
$$x = 5$$

Jill uses logic. She thinks about how addition and subtraction are related:

$x + 3 = 8$ means I have to add 3 to x to get 8.

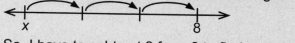

So, I have to subtract 3 from 8 to find x.

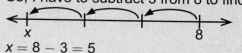

$$x = 8 - 3 = 5$$

1. Use Jill's method to solve the equation.

a) $x + 5 = 12$

$x = 12 - 5$

$x = 7$

b) $x + 3 = 10$

c) $x + 25 = 41$

d) $21 + x = 34$

e) $28 = 8 + x$

f) $41 = x + 14$

g) $17 + x = 56$

h) $x + 22 = 33$

i) $16 + x = 34$

j) $x + 35 = 61$

k) $6 + x = 100$

l) $5 + x + 2 = 18$

Mike and Jill solve the equation $x - 2 = 5$.

Mike uses preserving equality:

$$x - 2 = 5$$
$$x - 2 + 2 = 5 + 2$$
$$x = 7$$

Jill uses logic:

$x - 2 = 5$ means I have to subtract 2 from x to get 5.
So, I have to add 2 to 5 to find x.

$$x = 5 + 2 = 7$$

2. Use Jill's method to solve the equation.

a) $x - 5 = 12$

$x = 12 + 5$

$x = 17$

b) $x - 12 = 5$

c) $26 = x - 3$

d) $x - 19 = 9$

e) $x - 7 = 28$

f) $x - 13 = 22$

g) $14 = x - 27$

h) $29 = x - 32$

i) $x - 15 = 62$

j) $43 = x - 19$

k) $x - 51 = 49$

l) $73 = x - 21$

Examples: $12 \div 4 = \dfrac{12}{4}$ $15 \div 5 = \dfrac{15}{5}$ $x \div 3 = \dfrac{x}{3}$ $w \div 7 = \dfrac{w}{7}$

3. Solve the division problem.

a) $\dfrac{6}{3} = \boxed{2}$ b) $\dfrac{12}{6} = \boxed{}$ c) $\dfrac{12}{4} = \boxed{}$ d) $\dfrac{15}{5} = \boxed{}$

Mike and Jill solve the equation $3x = 12$.

Mike uses preserving equality:

$$3x = 12$$
$$3x \div 3 = 12 \div 3$$
$$x = 4$$

Jill uses logic:

$3x = 12$ means I have to multiply x by 3 to get 12.
So, I have to divide 12 by 3 to find x.

$$x = 12 \div 3 = 4$$

4. Use Mike's method to solve the equation by preserving equality.

a) $4x = 12$ b) $2x = 10$ c) $6x = 42$ d) $2x = 14$

$4x \div 4 = 12 \div 4$

$x = 3$

e) $7x = 28$ f) $6x = 18$ g) $7x = 49$ h) $8x = 48$

Mike and Jill solve the equation $\dfrac{x}{3} = 8$.

Mike uses preserving equality:

$$\dfrac{x}{3} = 8$$
$$\dfrac{x}{3} \times 3 = 8 \times 3$$
$$x = 24$$

Jill uses logic:

$\dfrac{x}{3} = 8$ means I have to divide x by 3 to get 8.

So, I have to multiply 8 by 3 to find x.

$x = 8 \times 3$, so $x = 24$

5. Solve the equation using logic.

a) $\dfrac{x}{2} = 3$ b) $2x = 8$ c) $\dfrac{x}{4} = 5$ d) $3 + x = 8$ e) $x - 5 = 6$

$x = 3 \times 2$

$x = 6$

f) $\dfrac{x}{3} = 4$ g) $5 + x = 12$ h) $12 = 2x$ i) $15 = 3x$ j) $4 = \dfrac{x}{5}$

k) $\dfrac{x}{7} = 4$ l) $\dfrac{x}{4} = 7$ m) $3x = 27$ n) $36 = 12x$ BONUS ▶ $\dfrac{x}{15} = 6$

50. The Four Quadrants of a Coordinate Grid

REMINDER ▶ Two numbers in order in brackets are called an ordered pair.
An ordered pair defines a point on a coordinate grid.
The point (0, 0) is called the origin.

$$A\ (4, 1) \qquad\qquad B\ (1, 4)$$

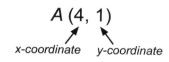
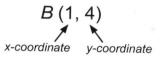
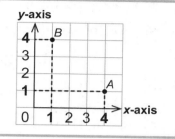

1. Fill in the coordinates for the given points.

A (_1_ , _3_)   B (,)   C (,)

D (,)   E (,)   F (,)

G (,)   H (,)   I (,)

J (,)   K (,)   L (,)

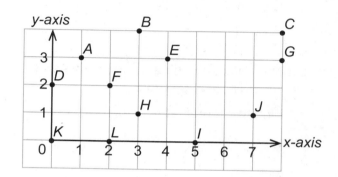

2. a) Mark the points on the number line.

$A\ 1.5 \qquad B\ 0.5 \qquad C\ 3\frac{1}{2} \qquad D\ 4\frac{1}{4}$

   b) Mark the points on the coordinate grid.

$A\ (0.5, 1.5) \qquad B\ (2.5, 1) \qquad C\ (4, 1.5)$

$D\ (5.5, 0.5) \qquad E\ (1\frac{1}{2}, 2) \qquad F\ (7, \frac{1}{2})$

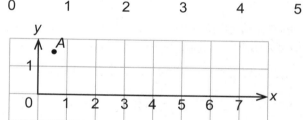

You can extend a grid to include negative numbers.
The **axes** are perpendicular lines that divide the grid
into four parts. These parts are called **quadrants**.

We use Roman numerals to number the quadrants.

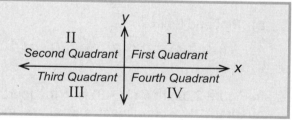

3. a) Label the origin (O), the x-axis, and the y-axis.

   b) Label the axes with positive and negative integers.

   c) Number the four quadrants (I, II, III, IV).

   d) Which quadrants are these points in?

   A (2, 2) ___I___   B (−2, −2) _____

   C (−2, 2) _____   D (2, −2) _____

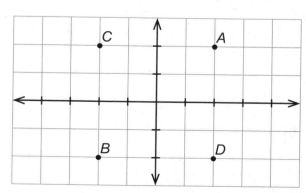

4. In Figure 1, point A (2, 3) is in the first quadrant. Its *x*- and *y*-coordinates are both **positive**.

   a) Find the coordinates of the points.

      P (,   )   Q (,   )

      R (,   )   S (,   )

   b) Plot and label.

      B (3, 2)   C (1, 4)   D (2, 6)

5. In Figure 1, point F (−2, 3) is in the second quadrant. Its *x*-coordinate is **negative** and its *y*-coordinate is **positive**.

   a) Find the coordinates of the points.

      K (,   )   L (,   )

      M (,   )   N (,   )

   b) Plot and label.

      G (−3, 2)   H (−2, 6)   I (−4, 3)

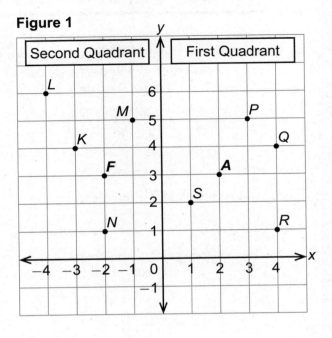

Figure 1

6. In Figure 2, point A (−2, −3) is in the third quadrant. Its *x*- and *y*-coordinates are both **negative**.

   a) Find the coordinates of the points.

      K (,   )   L (,   )

      M (,   )   N (,   )

   b) Plot and label.

      B (−3, −4)   C (−2, −6)   D (−4, −3)

7. In Figure 2, point F (2, −3) is in the fourth quadrant. Its *x*-coordinate is **positive** and its *y*-coordinate is **negative**.

   a) Find the coordinates of the points.

      P (,   )   Q (,   )

      R (,   )   S (,   )

   b) Plot and label.

      G (3, −4)   H (1, −6)

      I (4, −1)   J (4, −6)

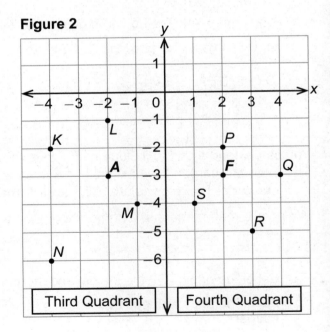

Figure 2

8. In Figure 3, points B (2, 0) and C (−4, 0) are both on the x-axis. The y-coordinate of any point on the x-axis is **zero**.

a) Find the coordinates of the points.

P (,   ) Q (,   )

b) Plot and label: A (5, 0), M (−2, 0)

9. In Figure 3, points D (0, 2) and E (0, −3) are both on the y-axis. The x-coordinate of any point on the y-axis is **zero**.

a) Plot and label: G (0, 4), H (0, −1).

b) Find the coordinates of the points.

K (,   ) L (,   )

Figure 3

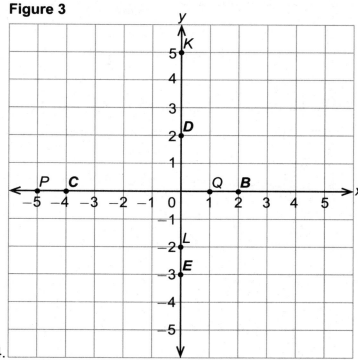

10. a) Find the coordinates of the points in Figure 4.

O (,   ) P (,   ) Q (,   ) R (,   ) S (,   )

T (,   ) U (,   ) V (,   ) W (,   )

b) Plot and label the points.

A (3, 4) B (5, −2) C (−3, −2)

D (−4, 1) E (3, 0) F (0, 2)

G (−5, 0) H (0, −4)

c) Sort the points in Figure 4 by location.

First Quadrant	A, R
Second Quadrant	
Third Quadrant	
Fourth Quadrant	
On the x-axis	
On the y-axis	
At the Origin	

Figure 4

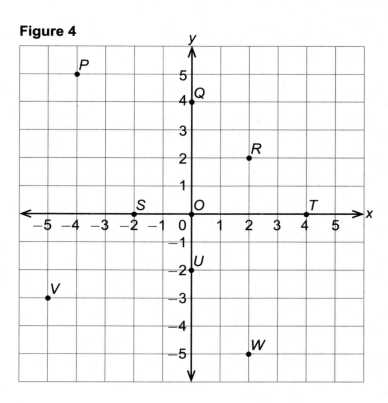

11. Which quadrant is each point in?

a) (−732, 805) _____   b) (732, −805) _____   c) (−732, −805) _____   d) (732, 805) _____

---

51. Coordinate Systems

1. Mark the points on the number line.

A 1.4 B −0.6 C $\frac{1}{2}$ D $-1\frac{2}{5}$ E −2.1 F $3\frac{2}{10}$

2. a) Find the coordinates of the points in Figure 1.

   $A (-4\frac{1}{2}, 1\frac{1}{2})$ $B (\quad , \quad)$

   $C (\quad , \quad)$ $D (\quad , \quad)$

   $E (\quad , \quad)$ $F (\quad , \quad)$

   $G (\quad , \quad)$ $H (\quad , \quad)$

   b) Plot and label the points.

   $I\,(4, 2)$ $J\,(3, -1)$

   $K\,(-1\frac{1}{2}, -1)$ $L\,(-2, \frac{1}{2})$ $M\,(1\frac{1}{2}, 0)$

   $N\,(0, 3\frac{1}{2})$ $O\,(-2\frac{1}{2}, -4\frac{1}{2})$ $P\,(-3\frac{1}{2}, 2\frac{1}{2})$

Figure 1

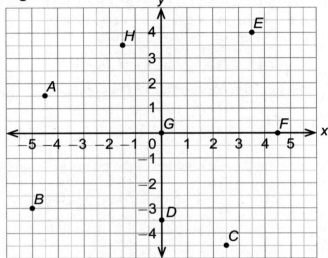

3. a) Draw lines parallel to the axes to find the coordinates of the points in Figure 2.

   $A (1\frac{1}{2}, -1\frac{1}{4})$ $B (\quad , \quad)$

   $C (\quad , \quad)$ $D (\quad , \quad)$

   $E (\quad , \quad)$ $F (\quad , \quad)$

   b) Plot and label the points.

   $G\,(3\frac{1}{4}, 0)$ $H\,(0, -1\frac{3}{4})$

   $I\,(-2\frac{3}{4}, 2)$ $J\,(3, -2\frac{1}{4})$

   $K\,(-2\frac{1}{2}, -2\frac{1}{2})$ $L\,(-1\frac{1}{2}, 2\frac{1}{2})$

Figure 2

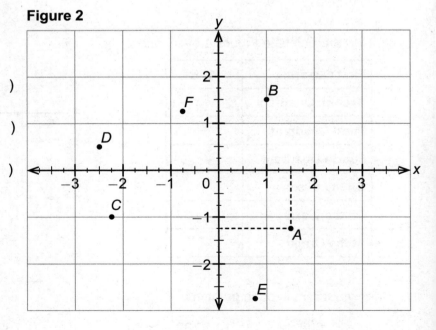

4. a) 2.7 cm = _____ mm 1.3 cm = _____ mm

b) Use a millimeter ruler to mark the points on the number line.

   P 2.7   Q −1.3

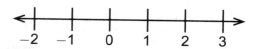

c) Draw lines parallel to the axes and measure the distance using a millimeter ruler to find the coordinates of the points in Figure 3.

Figure 3

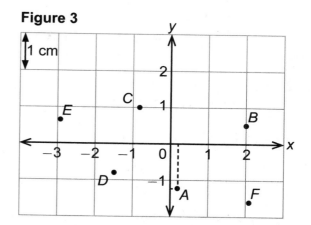

   A (0.2, −1.3) B (,   ) C (,   )

   D (,   ) E (,   ) F (,   )

d) Plot and label the points in Figure 3.

   G (−2.4, 2.8) H (1, 2.1)   I (1.3, −1)

   J (−2.5, −0.4) K (2.6, 1.9) L (−2.7, −1.2)

REMINDER ▶ We use Roman numerals to number quadrants.

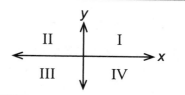

---

5. Which quadrant is the point in?

a) (−73.12, 80.5) __II__

b) (7.82, −8.55) _____

c) (−7.903, −.805) _____

d) (54.9, 435.98) _____

e) $(432\frac{167}{298}, -782\frac{91}{200})$ _____

f) $(-782\frac{91}{200}, 432\frac{167}{298})$ _____

6. Draw each point on the correct side of the correct axis (you don't have to show its exact position).

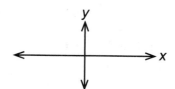

   A (0, 566.98)   B (−67.905, 0)   C $(0, -709\frac{1}{28})$ D $(90\frac{16}{29}, 0)$

7. Write the coordinates of two different points in each quadrant. Use decimals for one point and fractions for the other point.

a) Quadrant I: (,   ) (,   )

b) Quadrant II: (,   ) (,   )

c) Quadrant III: (,   ) (,   )

d) Quadrant IV :   (,   ) (,   )

---

52. Parallel Lines on a Grid

1. How many units **right** (⟶) or **left** (⟵) did the dot slide from position 1 to position 2?

a)
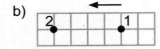

_____ units right

b)
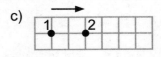

_____

c)

_____

2. How many units **right** or **left** and how many units **up** or **down** did the dot slide from position A to position B?

a)
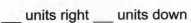

___ units right ___ units down

b)
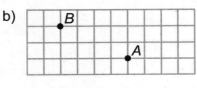

___ units left ___ units up

c)
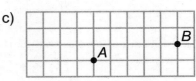

___ units right ___ unit up

3. Slide the dot.

a) 5 units right; 2 units down

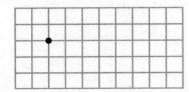

b) 6 units left; 3 units up

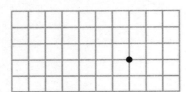

c) 3 units left; 4 units down

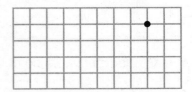

4. a) Slide both dots using the directions given. Draw a line segment between each dot and its image.

   i) 3 units right; 1 unit down

   ii) 5 units left; 2 units up

   iii) 6 units left; 2 units down

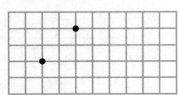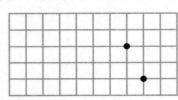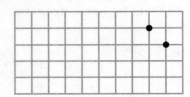

   b) Are the line segments you drew parallel? _____

5. a) Line segments AB and CD are parallel and equal. Describe the slide from A to B and from C to D. What do you notice?

   b) Join B to D and A to C. How many pairs of parallel sides does the quadrilateral ABDC have?

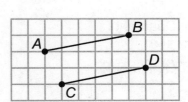

53. Coordinate Systems

1. Join the dots in the given column, row, or both.

a) Column 2

```
3  •  •  •
2  •  •  •
1  •  •  •
   1  2  3
```

b) Row 3

```
3  •  •  •
2  •  •  •
1  •  •  •
   1  2  3
```

c) Column 3, Row 1

```
3  •  •  •
2  •  •  •
1  •  •  •
   1  2  3
```

d) Column 1, Row 2

```
3  •  •  •
2  •  •  •
1  •  •  •
   1  2  3
```

2. Circle the dot in the given position.

a) Column 2, Row 1

```
3  •  •  •
2  •  •  •
1  •  ⊙  •
   1  2  3
```

b) Column 3, Row 2

```
3  •  •  •
2  •  •  •
1  •  •  •
   1  2  3
```

c) Column 3, Row 1

```
3  •  •  •
2  •  •  •
1  •  •  •
   1  2  3
```

d) Column 2, Row 2

```
3  •  •  •
2  •  •  •
1  •  •  •
   1  2  3
```

The row and the column for a point can be written in brackets.

The column is always written first.

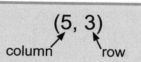

$(5, 3)$

column   row

3. Circle the dot in the given position.

a) (2, 1)

```
3  •  •  •
2  •  •  •
1  •  •  •
   1  2  3
```

b) (3, 3)

```
3  •  •  •
2  •  •  •
1  •  •  •
   1  2  3
```

c) (1, 2)

```
3  •  •  •
2  •  •  •
1  •  •  •
   1  2  3
```

d) (2, 3)

```
3  •  •  •
2  •  •  •
1  •  •  •
   1  2  3
```

You can use letters instead of numbers to label rows and columns.

4. Circle the given point.

a) (A, 3)

```
3  •  •  •
2  •  •  •
1  •  •  •
   A  B  C
```

b) (Y, B)

```
C  •  •  •
B  •  •  •
A  •  •  •
   X  Y  Z
```

c) (0, 2)

```
2  •  •  •
1  •  •  •
0  •  •  •
   0  1  2
```

d) (0, 0)

```
2  •  •  •
1  •  •  •
0  •  •  •
   0  1  2
```

e) (A, C)

```
D  •  •  •  •
C  •  •  •  •
B  •  •  •  •
A  •  •  •  •
   A  B  C  D
```

f) (2, X)

```
Z  •  •  •  •
Y  •  •  •  •
X  •  •  •  •
W  •  •  •  •
   1  2  3  4
```

g) (4, 1)

```
4  •  •  •  •
3  •  •  •  •
2  •  •  •  •
1  •  •  •  •
   1  2  3  4
```

h) (3, 4)

```
4  •  •  •  •
3  •  •  •  •
2  •  •  •  •
1  •  •  •  •
   1  2  3  4
```

Two numbers in brackets in order are called an **ordered pair.** The ordered pair that gives the position of a point on a grid is called the **coordinates** of the point.

5. a) Plot and label the points on the coordinate grid. Cross out the points as you go.

A (1, 5) B (1, 7) C (3, 7) D (6, 4)

E (7, 4) F (8, 3) G (7, 3) H (5, 1)

I (5, 0) J (4, 1) K (4, 2)

b) Join the points in alphabetical order. Then join A to K.

c) What does the picture you've got look like?

_____

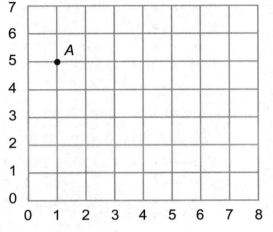

6. Graph each set of ordered pairs and join the dots to form a polygon. Identify the special quadrilateral drawn. The special quadrilaterals are parallelogram, rectangle, rhombus, trapezoid, square.

a) A (1, 2) B (4, 4) C (3, 2) D (0, 0)

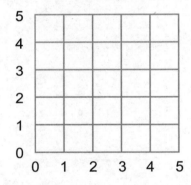

$ABCD$ is a _____.

b) E (3, 0) F (3, 5) G (1, 3) H (1, 1)

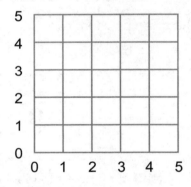

$EFGH$ is a _____.

7. a) Plot and label the points on the coordinate grid. Cross out the points as you go.

A (2, 1) B (5, 1) C (5, 4) D (2, 4)

E (9, 5) F (7, 6) G (0, 0) H (0, 3)

b) Join the correct points to make each quadrilateral, then identify it.

$ABCD$ _____

$BEFC$ _____

$ADHG$ _____

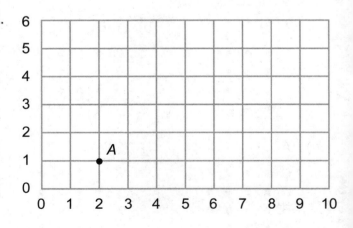

8. Write the coordinates of each point.

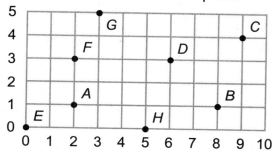

A (,   )   B (,   )

C (,   )   D (,   )

E (,   )   F (,   )

G (,   )   H (,   )

9. Add a point D so that the four points become the vertices of the given quadrilateral *ABCD*. Then write the coordinates of the vertices.

a) rectangle

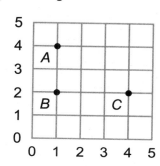

A (,   ), B (,   ),

C (,   ), D (,   )

b) a parallelogram

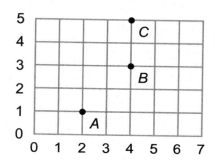

A (,   ), B (,   ),

C (,   ), D (,   )

10. Draw a quadrilateral of the given type on the grid. Write the coordinates of the vertices.

a) a trapezoid

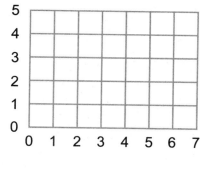

A (,   ), B (,   ),

C (,   ), D (,   )

b) a rhombus

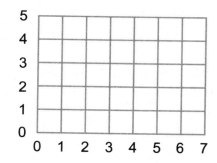

A (,   ), B (,   ),

C (,   ), D (,   )

BONUS ▶ Draw a polygon on a coordinate grid (use grid paper). Tell a partner the coordinates of the vertices of your polygon. Have your partner name the polygon.

54. Horizontal and Vertical Distance

1. a) Find the horizontal distance between the points.

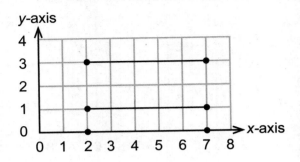

   i) (2, 0) and (7, 0): __5__ units

   ii) (2, 1) and (7, 1): _____ units

   iii) (2, 3) and (7, 3): _____ units

   iv) (2, y) and (7, y): _____ units

   b) How do you get the horizontal distance between the points from their first coordinates?

   _____

2. Find the difference between the first coordinates to find the horizontal distance between the points.

   a) (3, 0) and (1, 0): _____ units

   b) (5, 0) and (2, 0): _____ units

   c) (1, 10) and (8, 10): _____ units

   d) (8, 126) and (2, 126): _____ units

3. a) Find the vertical distance between the points.

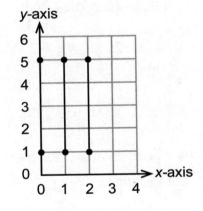

   i) (0, 2) and (0, 5): _____ units

   ii) (1, 2) and (1, 5): _____ units

   iii) (2, 2) and (2, 5): _____ units

   iv) (x, 2) and (x, 5): _____ units

   b) How do you get the vertical distance between the points from their second coordinates?

   _____

   _____

4. Find the difference between the second coordinates to find the vertical distance between the points.

   a) (1, 3) and (1, 2): _____ units

   b) (1, 5) and (1, 2): _____ units

   c) (10, 10) and (10, 2): _____ units

   d) (4, 5) and (4, 2): _____ units

   e) (14, 2) and (14, 7): _____ units

   f) (561, 2) and (561, 5): _____ units

5. The diagram at right shows a coordinate grid with some lines and labels left out. A is at (5, 5). The vertical distance between A and D is 5.

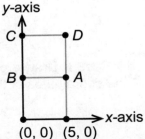

   Write the coordinates of B, C, and D:

   B (,   )   C (,   )   D (,   )

55. Ratios and Coordinate Systems

1. Make a ratio table for each ratio.

a) 3:5

3	5
6	10
9	15

b) 7:2

c) 4:9

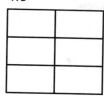

BONUS ▶ 12:7

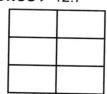

2. Make a ratio table. Then write a list of ordered pairs for each table.

a) 3:7

3	7	(3, 7)
6	14	(6, 14)
9	21	(,)

b) 11:5

c) 5:6

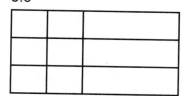

3. a) Write a list of ordered pairs for each ratio table.

i)

1	2	(1, 2)
2	4	(,)
3	6	(,)
4	8	(,)

ii)

1	1	
2	2	
3	3	
4	4	

iii)

3	1	
6	2	
9	3	
12	4	

b) Mark the ordered pairs on the graph and connect the points.

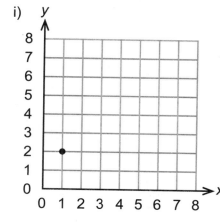

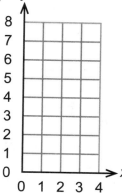

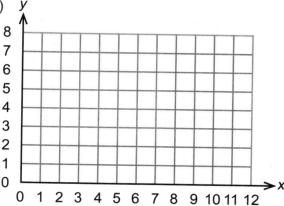

c) What do you notice about the points in each graph? _____

d) Extend the line to the edges of the grid. What is the lowest point on the line that is on the grid?

i) (,)   ii) (,)   iii) (,)

What do you notice? _____

When you plot the ordered pairs from a ratio table, connect the dots, and extend the line, the line will always pass through (0, 0).

4. a) Finish the ratio table. Then plot the ordered pairs. Pay attention to the scale!

i)

x	y
4	3

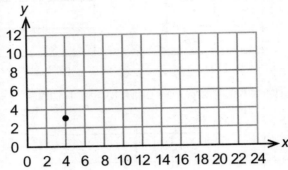

ii)

x	y
5	2

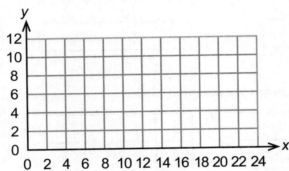

iii)

x	y
6	4

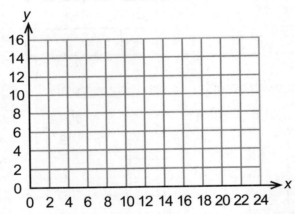

b) Join the points on each graph with a line. Extend the line to make sure the lines go through (0, 0).

5. a) Plot the ordered pairs from each table. Connect the points and extend the line.

i)

Input	Output
1	1
2	3
3	5

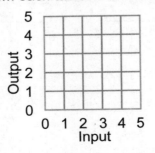

ii)

Input	Output
1	2
2	3
3	4

b) How can you tell from the graph that these are not ratio tables?

JUMP Math Accumula

56. Equivalent Expressions

1. Complete the table, and then answer the question.

a)

n	$3n$	$n + n + n$
1	$3(1) = 3$	$1 + 1 + 1 = 3$
2	$3(2) = 6$	$2 + 2 + 2 = 6$
3		
4		

Do $3n$ and $n + n + n$ have equal values for every n in the table? _____

b)

n	$2n + 2$	$2 \times (n + 1)$
1	$2(1) + 2 = 4$	$2 \times (1 + 1) = 4$
2		
3		
4		

Do $2n + 2$ and $2 \times (n + 1)$ have equal values for every n in the table? _____

2. Find the number that makes each equation true. Write the numbers in the boxes, and then write a variable for the last equation.

a) $3 \times 1 = \boxed{1} \times 3$

$3 \times 2 = \boxed{} \times 3$

$3 \times 3 = \boxed{} \times 3$

$3 \times 7 = \boxed{} \times 3$

$3 \times n = \boxed{} \times 3$

b) $1 + 2 = 2 + \boxed{1}$

$2 + 2 = 2 + \boxed{}$

$3 + 2 = 2 + \boxed{}$

$9 + 2 = 2 + \boxed{}$

$n + 2 = 2 + \boxed{}$

c) $1 + 1 + 1 = 3 \times \boxed{1}$

$2 + 2 + 2 = 3 \times \boxed{}$

$3 + 3 + 3 = 3 \times \boxed{}$

$8 + 8 + 8 = 3 \times \boxed{}$

$n + n + n = 3 \times \boxed{}$

d) $2 \times 1 - 1 = \boxed{1}$

$2 \times 2 - 2 = \boxed{}$

$2 \times 3 - 3 = \boxed{}$

$2 \times 4 - 4 = \boxed{}$

$2 \times n - n = \boxed{}$

3. Write an addition equation and a multiplication equation for the area of the figure.

a)

$5 + 5 + 5 = $ _____

$3 \times 5 = $ _____

b)

_____

_____

c)

$4 + 4 + 4 = $ _____

$4 \times 3 = $ _____

d)

_____

_____

These two figures have equal areas: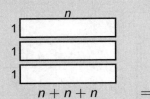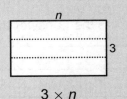

$$n + n + n \quad = \quad 3 \times n$$

The expressions $n + n + n$ and $3n$ are **equivalent expressions** because they have the same value for all n's.

4. Use the figures to write equivalent expressions.

a)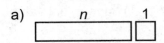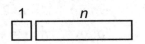

b)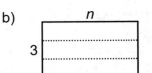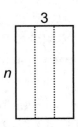

$$\underline{\quad n + 1 \quad} = \underline{\quad 1 + n \quad} \qquad \underline{\hspace{3cm}} = \underline{\hspace{3cm}}$$

c)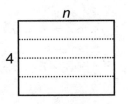

BONUS ▶

 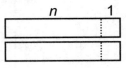 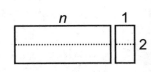

$$\underline{\hspace{3cm}} = \underline{\hspace{3cm}} \qquad \underline{\quad 2 \times (n + 1) \quad} = \underline{\hspace{3cm}}$$

Jeff puts two shapes together.

Jeff notices that $3 \times n + 3 \times 2 = 3 \times (n + 2)$. This shows the distributive property for algebraic expressions.

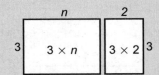 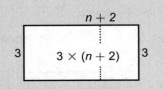

5. Use the distributive property to write an equivalent expression.

a) $4 \times (x - 3)$

$= 4 \times x - 4 \times 3$

$= 4x - 12$

So, $4 \times (x - 3)$ and $\underline{\; 4x - 12 \;}$ are equivalent.

b) $5 \times (n + 3)$

$=$

$=$

So, $5 \times (n + 3)$ and $\underline{\hspace{2cm}}$ are equivalent.

c) $(2 + t) \times 6$

BONUS ▶ $(5 - 3) \times x$

6. Use the distributive property to write an equivalent expression.

a) $3x + 6$

$= \underline{\; 3 \;} \times (\underline{\hspace{1cm}} + \underline{\hspace{1cm}})$

b) $4x + 12$

$= \underline{\hspace{1cm}} \times (\underline{\hspace{1cm}} + \underline{\hspace{1cm}})$

c) $10y + 15$

$= \underline{\hspace{1cm}} \times (\underline{\hspace{1cm}} + \underline{\hspace{1cm}})$

57. Solving Algebraic Equations

The expression 5×2 is short for $2 + 2 + 2 + 2 + 2$.
Similarly, the expression $5x$ is short for $x + x + x + x + x$.

$$\underbrace{x + x + x + x + x} = \underbrace{x + x} + \underbrace{x + x + x}$$
$$5x \qquad = \quad 2x \quad + \quad 3x$$

$5x$ and $2x + 3x$ are equivalent expressions. In the expression $5x$, the number 5 is called the **coefficient**.

1. Circle the coefficients in each expression.

a) ⑦w

b) $0.5k - 11y$

c) $2x - 5y$

d) $-6.1z + \dfrac{3}{4}q$

2. Write three equivalent expressions for $6x$.

$6x = \underbrace{x + x + x} + \underbrace{x + x + x}$
$6x = \quad 3x \quad + \quad 3x$

$6x = \underbrace{x + x} + \underbrace{x + x + x + x}$
$6x = \qquad +$

$6x = \underbrace{x + x} + \underbrace{x + x + x + x}$
$6x = \quad +$

3. Add by adding the coefficients.

a) $3x + 5x = \underline{\quad 8x \quad}$

b) $5x + 3x = \underline{\qquad}$

c) $7x + x = \underline{\qquad}$

d) $5x + 6x = \underline{\qquad}$

e) $19x + x = \underline{\qquad}$

BONUS ▶ $2x + 5x + 4x = \underline{\qquad}$

4. Group the x's together, and then solve the equation for x.

a) $2x + 5x = 21$

b) $3x + 2x = 15$

c) $6x + x = 28$

$7x = 21$

$x = \dfrac{21}{7} = 3$

d) $4x + 5x = 18$

e) $8x + 3x = 22$

BONUS ▶ $5x + 2x = 0$

5. Fill in the blank.

a) $3 - 3 = \underline{\qquad}$

b) $8 - 8 = \underline{\qquad}$

c) $132 - 132 = \underline{\qquad}$

d) $3.1 - 3.1 = \underline{\qquad}$

e) $\dfrac{1}{2} - \dfrac{1}{2} = \underline{\qquad}$

f) $2\dfrac{1}{3} - 2\dfrac{1}{3} = \underline{\qquad}$

g) $1.53 - 1.53 = \underline{\qquad}$

h) $\dfrac{4}{3} - \dfrac{4}{3} = \underline{\qquad}$

i) $x - x = \underline{\qquad}$

j) $\dfrac{3}{5} + 3 - 3 = \underline{\qquad}$

k) $5\dfrac{1}{4} + 3 - 3 = \underline{\qquad}$

l) $x + 3 - 3 = \underline{\qquad}$

Every time you see a number or variable subtracted from itself in an equation (For example: $3 - 3$, $5 - 5$, $8 - 8$, $x - x$), you can cross out both numbers or variables because they will add to 0. Crossing out parts of an equation that make 0 is called **cancelling**.

6. Fill in the blank by crossing out numbers or variables that add to 0.

a) $4 + \not{3} - \not{3} = \underline{\quad 4 \quad}$

b) $5 + 2 - 2 = \underline{\quad\quad}$

c) $7 + 1 - 1 = \underline{\quad\quad}$

d) $8 + 6.2 - 6.2 = \underline{\quad\quad}$

e) $\frac{1}{2} + 7 - \frac{1}{2} = \underline{\quad\quad}$

f) $\frac{7}{3} + 9 - \frac{7}{3} = \underline{\quad\quad}$

g) $4 + 3 - 3 + 7 - 7 = \underline{\quad\quad}$

h) $0.5 + 2 - 2 + 4 - 0.5 = \underline{\quad\quad}$

i) $7 + x - 7 = \underline{\quad\quad}$

j) $x + 129 - 129 = \underline{\quad\quad}$

k) $x + 4.6 - 4.6 = \underline{\quad\quad}$

l) $x + n - n = \underline{\quad\quad}$

7. Rewrite the expression as a sum of individual variables and then cancel. Write what's left.

a) $5x - 2x = \underline{\quad 3x \quad}$

$x + x + x + \not{x} + \not{x} - \not{x} - \not{x}$

b) $4x - x = \underline{\quad\quad}$

c) $5x - x + 2x = \underline{\quad\quad}$

8. Subtract by subtracting the coefficients.

a) $7x - 5x = \underline{\quad\quad}$

b) $8x - 4x = \underline{\quad\quad}$

c) $4x - 2x + 3x = \underline{\quad\quad}$

d) $9x - 3x + 4x = \underline{\quad\quad}$

e) $7x - 5x + x = \underline{\quad\quad}$

f) $5x - 5x + 2x = \underline{\quad\quad}$

9. Group the x's together, and then solve for x.

a) $8x - 3x + x = 30$

b) $5x + x - x - 2x = 0.21$

c) $7x - 3x - 2x = 2.2$

d) $1.4 = 4x - x + x + 3x$

e) $9x - 2x - 2x = 2$

f) $3.2 = 4x + 3x - 3x - 4x + 4x$

10. Solve for x. Check your answer.

a) $\quad x + 0.3 = 1.5$

$x + 0.3 - 0.3 = 1.5 - 0.3$

$x = 1.2$

Check by replacing x with
your answer: $1.2 + 0.3 = \mathbf{1.5} \checkmark$

b) $\quad x - 0.4 = 2$

$x - 0.4 + 0.4 = 2 + 0.4$

c) $\quad 1.5 + x = 1.9$

d) $3.1 = x + 1.4$

e) $0.9 = x - 4.6$

f) $2x = 4.6$

g) $0.8x = 5.6$

h) $1.5x = 15$

i) $1.1x = 4.4$

58. Word Problems

To solve word problems, you turn the words into algebraic expressions. The words give clues to the operations you need to use. Here are some of the clues for different operations:

Add	Subtract	Multiply	Divide
increased by	less than	product	divided by
sum	difference	times	divided into
more than	decreased by	twice as many	
	reduced by		

1. Match each algebraic expression with the correct description.

2 more than a number	$4x$	2 divided into a number	$3x$
a number divided by 3	$x - 2$	a number reduced by 4	$x \div 2$
2 less than a number	$x + 2$	a number times 3	$x + 3$
the product of a number and 4	$x - 3$	twice as many as a number	$x - 4$
a number decreased by 3	$x \div 3$	a number increased by 3	$2x$

2. Write an algebraic expression for the description.

a) four more than a number

b) a number decreased by 8.5

c) a number divided by 8

d) two less than a number

e) a number increased by 2.9

f) a number reduced by 4

g) five times a number

h) 6 divided into a number

i) the product of 7 and a number

j) twice as many as a number

k) the sum of a number and 4.7

l) the product of a number and 3.3

When solving word problems, the word "is" translates to the equal sign, "=".

Example: "Two more than a number is seven" can be written as $x + 2 = 7$.

3. Solve the problem by first writing an equation.

a) Four more than a number is eighteen.

b) Five less than a number is 12.4.

c) Five times a number is thirty.

d) Six times a number is forty-two.

e) Six divided into a number is 1.5.

f) The product of a number and 5 is two.

g) A number multiplied by two is thirty-six.

h) A number multiplied by three is eighteen.

i) Three divided into a number is 2.3.

j) Twice a number is 10.6.

k) Three times a number is 3.6.

BONUS ▶ Half of a number is 1 more than 4.

4. a) Write an expression for the perimeter of the shape (*x* stands for the length of the unknown sides). Then write an equivalent expression for the perimeter.

i)

ii)

iii)

$x + x + x = 3x$

b) The perimeter of each shape in part a) is 12. Find the unknown side lengths.

5. Write an equation to find the length of the missing side.

a)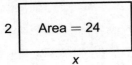

b)

c)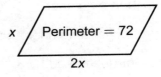

6. Mark's dad is three times older than Mark. The difference between their ages is 24 years. How old is Mark?

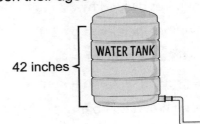

7. The height of the water in a water tank is 42 inches. The height of the water in the tank decreases 6 inches each day. After how many days will the water tank be empty?

42 inches

8. The sum of two numbers is 45. One number is twice the other number. Write an equation and find the numbers.

9. Chandra is five times as old as Rita. The sum of their ages is 42. How old are Chandra and Rita?

BONUS ▶ Binh paid $51 for two pairs of pants. He bought the first pair at the regular price, but the second pair at half price. What is the regular price for one pair of pants? Hint: Let *x* be the price of the second pair.

JUMP Math Accumula

59. Graphs and Equations

1. For each set of points, write a list of ordered pairs and complete the table. Then write an equation that tells you the relationship between *x* and *y*.

a)

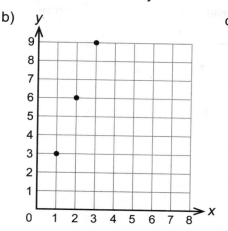

b)

c)

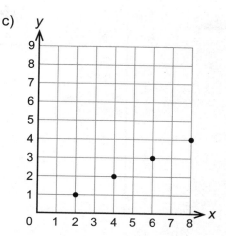

Ordered Pairs	x	y
(1 , 2)	1	2
(,)		
(,)		
(,)		

$2 \times x = y$

$or\ y = 2x$

Ordered Pairs	x	y
(,)		
(,)		
(,)		
(,)		

Ordered Pairs	x	y
(,)		
(,)		
(,)		
(,)		

2. Complete the table and plot the points on the grid for the given rule.

a) Multiply by 2 and add 1

x	$2x + 1 = y$
1	$2 \times 1 + 1 = 3$
2	$2 \times 2 + 1 = 5$
3	
4	

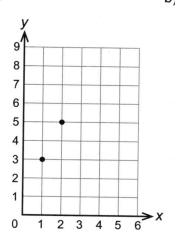

b) Multiply by 3 and subtract 3

x	$3x - 3 = y$
1	
2	
3	
4	

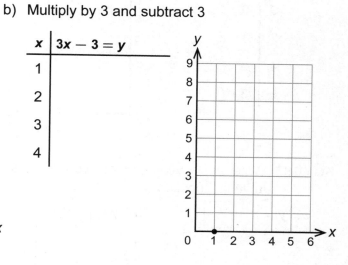

3. Draw a coordinate grid (like those above) on grid paper and plot the following ordered pairs: (1, 3), (3, 5), (5, 7), and (7, 9).

4. Make a table for each set of points on the coordinate grid. Write a rule for each table that tells you how to calculate y from x.

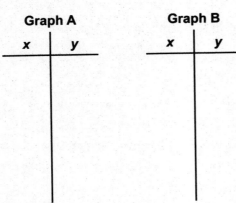

Graph A

x	y

Graph B

x	y

Graph C

x	y

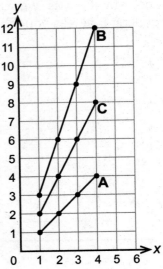

Rule: $y =$ ____ $y =$ ____ $y =$ ____

5. Write a list of ordered pairs based on the table provided. Plot the ordered pairs on the graph and connect the points to form a line.

a)

x	y
0	1	(,)
1	2	(,)
2	3	(,)
3	4	(,)

b)

x	y
0	0	(,)
1	2	(,)
2	4	(,)
3	6	(,)

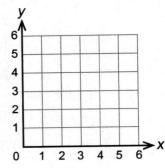

c)

x	y
0	0	(,)
2	1	(,)
4	2	(,)
6	3	(,)

d)

x	y
1	0	(,)
2	1	(,)
3	2	(,)
4	3	(,)

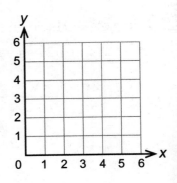

BONUS ▶ Write an equation that tells you the relationship between x and y for each table in Question 5.

a) $y = x +$ ☐   b) $y =$ ☐x c) $y =$ d) $y =$

60. Dependent and Independent Variables

1. The graph shows the cost of making an international phone call with a cell phone company.

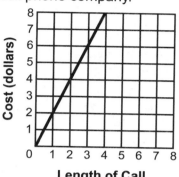

Cost (dollars) vs Length of Call (minutes)

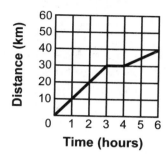

a) If you talked for 2 minutes, how much would you pay?

b) What is the cost for a 1 minute call?

c) How much would you pay to talk for 10 minutes?

2. The graph shows the distance Kathy traveled on a cycling trip.

Distance (km) vs Time (hours)

a) How far had Kathy cycled after 2 hours?

b) How far had Kathy traveled after 6 hours?

c) Did Kathy rest at all on her trip? How do you know?

In an equation with two variables, the **dependent variable** represents the output or effect and the **independent variable** represents the input or cause.

Example: In Question 1, the length of the call is the independent variable and the cost is the dependent variable because the cost depends on the length of call.

Mathematicians usually use the *x*-axis for independent variables and the *y*-axis for dependent variables.

---

3. Tom runs a 120 meter race.

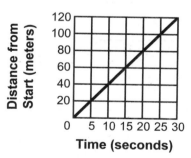

Distance from Start (meters) vs Time (seconds)

a) What are the dependent and independent variables?

b) How far from the start was Tom after

   i) 10 seconds?   ii) 25 seconds?

c) If he continues running at the same rate, how far will Tom be after 1 minute?

4. The graph shows the cost of renting a bike from Mika's store.

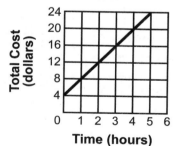

Total Cost (dollars) vs Time (hours)

a) What are the dependent and independent variables?

b) How much would you pay to rent the bike for

   i) 2 hours?   ii) 4 hours?   iii) 3 hours?

c) How much do you pay for the bike before you have even ridden it?

5. For each table below, write a rule that tells

  • how the input changes,
  • how the output changes, and
  • the relation between the input and output.

Example:

Input	Output
1	3
2	6
3	9
4	12

• The numbers in the input column increase by 1 each time.
• The numbers in the output column increase by 3 each time.
• Multiply the input by 3 to get the output.

a)

Input	Output
1	6
2	12
3	18

b)

Input	Output
1	9
2	18
3	27

c)

Input	Output
1	11
2	22
3	33

d)

Input	Output
1	7
2	14
3	21

e)

Input	2.5	3.0	4.0	5.5	7.5	10.0	13.0
Output	5	6	8	11	15	20	26

f)

Input	1	2	3	4	5	6	7
Output	1	4	9	16	25	36	49

g)

Input	1	2	3	4	5	6	7
Output	2.1	4.2	6.3	8.4	10.5	12.6	14.7

6. The table shows the number of kilometers Janelle can run in 15 minutes. Complete the table. Note: Assume she keeps running at the same rate.

Distance	Time (seconds)	Time (minutes)	Time (hours)
2.3 km		15	$\frac{1}{4}$
4.6 km			
	2,700		

61. Introduction to Inequalities

Tan weighs 80 pounds, and Walter weighs more than 80 pounds. If w is Walter's weight, then the **inequality** $80 < w$ represents what we know about Walter's weight.

Walter's weight could be 90 pounds (90 is more than 80), so 90 is one **solution** for the inequality $80 < w$.

We can use a number line to show the inequality.

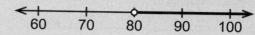

- The thick black part of the number line shows all the possible solutions.
- There is a white circle at 80 because Walter's weight cannot be 80 ($80 < 80$ is not correct).

1. Write an inequality for the phrase.

   a) w is less than 7.   ___$w < 7$___

   b) w is greater than 50.   _____

   c) w is less than 0.   _____

   d) w is greater than −5.   _____

   e) w is less than −7.   _____

   f) w is greater than 0.   _____

2. Write the meaning of the inequality.

   a) $w < 5$ __w is less than 5.__

   b) $w > -4$ _____

   c) $w > 0$ _____

   d) $w < -5$ _____

Every inequality can be written in two ways. For example, the inequality "w is greater than 80" can be written as "80 is less than w."

3. Write the inequality in another way.

   a) w is less than 20.   __20 is greater than w.__

   b) w is greater than 4.   _____

   c) w is greater than 0.   _____

   d) w is greater than −5.   _____

4. Circle the numbers that are solutions for the inequality $80 < b$.

   75   91   81   69   93.5   79.9   80.5   100   80

5. Connect each inequality on top to its solutions on the bottom.
   Note: Each inequality has more than one solution.

   $x < 5$ $x < 0$ $10 < x$

   3   15   −2   5   −5   23   10

6. Write an inequality for the number line.

a)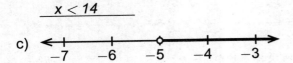

      <u>$x < 14$</u>

b)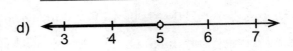

      _____

c)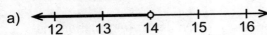

      _____

d)

      _____

7. Write an inequality for the story. Let x represent the unknown. If the solution is always a positive number, write "and $x > 0$."

a) Susan is 12 years old. Susan's sister is younger than Susan.

      <u>$x < 12$ and $x > 0$</u>

b) Julius has $7.50 and Michael has less money than Julius.

      _____

c) The temperature will be less than 12 degrees on Sunday.

      _____

d) Tyrone is younger than his 17-year-old brother.

      _____

8. Draw a thick line to show the solution of the inequality on the given number line. Part a) is done for you.

a) $x < 9$

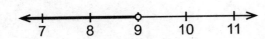

b) $x > 17$

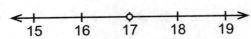

c) $x > 0$

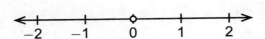

d) $x < -4$

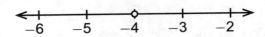

BONUS ▶ Malina is going shopping. She plans to buy a shirt for $7, a pair of pants for $15, and a pair of shoes that is more expensive than the pair of pants. Write an inequality to represent the amount of money that she needs to pay for the items. Show the inequality on a number line.

       JUMP Math Accumula